FLAGS OF THE CONFEDERACY
AN ILLUSTRATED HISTORY

THE FLAGS OF THE CONFEDERACY
AN ILLUSTRATED HISTORY

BY

Devereaux D. Cannon, Jr.

St. Lukes Press
and
Broadfoot Publishing

1988

Library of Congress Cataloging in Publication Data
Cannon, Devereaux D., Jr. 1954

THE FLAGS OF THE CONFEDERACY
        Includes Index
            1. Flags—Confederate States of America
I. Title.
CR113.5058 1988 929.9' 2' 0975 87-38122
ISBN 0-918518-62-8 (pbk.)
ISBN 0-918518-63-6

Cover Design by Larry Pardue

This book is dedicated to
DEVEREAUX D. CANNON, III
whose enthusiasm is unbounded,
and to his mother,
who has the patience to put up with
two unreconstructed rebels.

ACKNOWLEDGEMENTS

Special thanks are due to the following individuals and institutions who rendered invaluable assistance in the preparation of this book:

Nora T. Cannon, Esquire, Nashville, Tennessee;

Mark Lea "Beau" Cantrell, Esquire, El Reno, Oklahoma for assistance on flags in the Trans-Mississippi Department;

Confederate Research Center, Hill College History Complex, Hillsboro, Texas

John Hudson, Tennessee State Museum, Nashville, Tennessee;

Timothy Kelly, Nashville, Tennessee;

Howard Michael Madaus, Milwaukee Public Museum, Milwaukee, Wisconsin for general assistance on a variety of details;

Dr. John McGlone, Tennessee State Library and Archives, Nashville, Tennessee;

Bill Pitts, Confederate Memorial Hall, Oklahoma Historical Society, Oklahoma City, Oklahoma;

Col. Frank R. Rankin, Louisville, Kentucky for information on the Kentucky seal; and

Rebecca R. Tickle, Lucy, Tennessee.

Table of Contents

Chapter 1: In the Beginning . . . Flags.. 1-4
Chapter 2: "Stars and Bars".. 7-13
Chapter 3: "Stainless Banner".. 14-21
Chapter 4: The Confederate Flag—Final Edition........................... 22-24
Chapter 5: Evolution of the Flag... 25-28
Chapter 6: The Bonnie Blue Flag... 31-33
Chapter 7: State Flags.. 34-48
Chapter 8: Battle Flags.. 51-65
Chapter 9: The Flag at Sea... 66-72
Epilogue... 73
Further Reading... 75-76
Appendix A: Chronology.. 77-85
Appendix B: Confederate Flag Laws... 86-90
Appendix C: Confederate Flag Day and The Salute
to the Confederate Flag.. 91
A Confederate Anthem: "The Bonnie Blue Flag"........................... 92-95
Index... 96-98

List of Illustrations

Figure 1.   Proposed Flag of the Confederate States, Submitted to Congress   March 4, 1861 by William Porcher Miles.

Figure 2-3. Two of the Flags Submitted to the Provisional Congress on March 4, 1861.

Figure 4.   Flag of the Confederate States of America Adopted by the Provisional Congress. March 4, 1861.

Figure 5-7. Three Flag Designs Submitted to the Provisional Congress by Nicola Marschall.

Figure 8.   Specifications of a Representative Example of the "Stars and Bars."

Figure 9.   Flag Proposal of the Joint Committee on Flag and Seal—April 19, 1862.

Figure 10.   Original Version of the Flag in Senate Bill No. 132, 1863.

Figure 11.   A Proposed Amendment of Senate Bill No. 132, 1863.

Figure 12.   Congressman Swan's Proposed Amendment to Senate Bill No. 132.

Figure 13.   Flag of the Confederate States of America, May 1, 1863 to March 4, 1865.

Figure 14.   Confederate States Treasury Note Decorated with the Confederate Flag and a Portrait of Stonewall Jackson.

Figure 15.   Detailed Specifications for the Construction of the Stainless Banner.

Figure 16.   Flag of the Confederate States of America Since March 4, 1865.

Figure 17.   Detailed Specifications for the Construction of the Last Confederate Flag.

Figure 18.   St. George's Cross of England.

Figure 19.   St. Andrew's Cross of Scotland.

Figure 20.   Union Flag of Great Britain 1606-1801.

Figure 21.   British Red Ensign Prior to 1801.

Figure 22.   Flag of the United States 1776-1777.

Figure 23.   Flag of the United States 1777-1795.

Figure 24.   The Bonnie Blue Flag.

Figure 25.   Flag of South Carolina, January 26, 1861 to January 28, 1861.

Figure 26.   Flag of South Carolina, January 26, 1861 to Present.

Figure 27.   Flag of Mississippi Adopted January 26, 1861.

Figure 28.   Provisional Flag of Florida, January 13, 1861 to September 13, 1861.

Figure 29.   Flag of Florida Adopted September 13, 1861.

Figure 30.   Flag of Alabama.

Figure 31.   Reverse of the Alabama State Flag.

Figure 32.   Flag of Georgia.

Figure 33.   Pelican Flag.

Figure 34.   Flag of Louisiana Adopted February 11, 1861.

Figure 35.   Flag of the Texas Revolution, 1835.

Figure 36.   Texas Flag, March 11, 1836 to December 10, 1836.

Figure 37.   Texas Flag, December 10, 1836 to January 25, 1839; and Unofficial Variant
                of the Alabama State Flag, 1861.

Figure 38.   Texas Flag January 25, 1839 to Present.

Figure 39.   Texas Naval Ensign.

figure 40.   Texas Civil Ensign.

Figure 41.   Virginia State Flag.

Figure 42.   North Carolina State Flag.

Figure 43.   Proposed Tennessee State Flag, 1861.

Figure 44.   The Seal of the State of Kentucky.

Figure 45.   Flag of Missouri.

Figure 46.   General Beauregard's Prototype of the Battle Flag.

Figure 47.   Silk Battle Flag Issued November 1861.

Figure 48.   First Bunting Issue, 1862, Army of Northern Virginia.

Figure 49.   Third Bunting Issue, 1863, Army of Northern Virginia.

Figure 50.   Hardee's Corps, Army of Tennessee.

Figure 51.   Polk's Corps Battle Flag, Army of Tennessee.

Figure 52.   Bragg's Corps Battle Flag, Army of the Mississippi, First Pattern.

Figure 53.   Bragg's Corps Battle Flag, Army of the Mississippi, Second Pattern.

Figure 54.   Army of Tennessee Battle Flag, 1864.

Figure 55.   Battle Flag of the Department of South Carolina, Georgia and Florida.

Figure 56.   Battle Flag of the Department of East Tennessee.

Figure 57.   Battle Flag of the Department of Alabama, Mississippi, and East Louisiana.

Figure 58.   Battle Flag of Shelby's Brigade.

Figure 59.   Battle flag of Parson's Texas Calvary.

Figure 60.   Battle Flag of General Richard Taylor's Army.

Figure 61.   Trans-Mississippi Department, Van Dorn's Corps.

Figure 62.   Trans-Mississippi Department, The "Missouri Battle Flag."

Figure 63.   Trans-Mississippi Department, Cherokee Nation.

Figure 64.   Flag of the Choctaw Brigade.

Figure 65.   Illustration of a Three Masted Ship Demonstrating Placement
of the Ensign, Jack and Commission Pennant.

Figure 66.   Confederate States Naval Ensign After May 26, 1863.

Figure 67.   Confederate Navy Jack March 4, 1861 to May 26, 1863.

Figure 68.   Confederate Navy Jack after May 26, 1863.

Figure 69.   Confederate Commission Pennant, March 4, 1861 to May 26, 1863.

Figure 70.   Confederate Commission Pennant, After May 26, 1863.

Figure 71.   Variant Confederate Commission Pennant Used After May 1, 1863.

Figure 72.   Confederate States Revenue Service Ensign.

FLAGS OF THE CONFEDERACY
AN ILLUSTRATED HISTORY

CHAPTER 1
IN THE BEGINNING . . . FLAGS

Flags are fond symbols, popular with people of all ages. They can be just pretty pieces of colored bunting snapping in the breeze to give an event a festive air, or they can be the charismatic expression of a cause.

National flags are the history and glory of a people expressed in the art of the seamstress. The flags of States which are members of a federation are more difficult to deal with on so general a basis. As an expression of the sovereignty of each member State, they tend, in happy times, to be lost in the patriotism felt for the federation and symbolized in its flag. Regardless of politics, battle flags, while they existed for the ordinary and necessary purposes of recognition and the direction of armies, came to be totems. For the soldiers who followed them, they acquired a personality of their own and often became the object of battle, rather than its markers. In the Confederate States of America, which had an independent political existence of only four years before they were conquered and reincorporated into the United States, all these variations found full play.

All revolutionary movements breed a wide variety of flags. This was certainly true in the early days of the Southern independence movement, and it would continue to be true for the military forces of the Confederacy in the Western and Trans-Mississippi theatres. Yet the Confederate revolution was a conservative revolution in that the forms of government remained intact in the States, and the new federal government established by them was almost a carbon copy of that from which they had separated. In part as a result of the conservative and legalistic manner in which the Confederacy was established, the first national flag of the Confederate States was adopted sooner and promulgated in a more uniform and regular manner than is usual with flags associated with other revolutions.

In order to have a good understanding of the Confederate flags in this book, it is helpful to have an understanding of the civil and political structure of the Confederate States government. When the Southern States seceded from the United States of America in 1860 and 1861, they believed that they were acting in a perfectly legal and acceptable manner. The Constitution of 1787 had been drafted by delegates from the States and had been voluntarily ratified by the people of the several States. No State had been forced into the union, and any State whose people did not wish to join the union could go its own way. Logically, it followed therefore that any State could also voluntarily leave the union when its people believed that the union was no longer serving its purpose of establishing justice and/or insuring domestic tranquility.

Secession did not change the State governments in their internal operations, and they continued to function in their daily activities. It was recognized, however, that the purposes for which the old union had been formed in 1788 were good, and that the failure of the system in 1860 could be remedied by the formation of a new and southern confederacy. Accordingly, the newly independent States called a convention to form a new federal government.

The Convention met in Montgomery, Alabama on February 4, 1861 where the Confederate founding fathers proceded to form a provisional or temporary government to preside over the new country until a permanent government could be established. The Convention also drafted a new Constitution very similar to the United States Constitution and created the machinery for the establishment of a permanent government a year later. After toying with the names "Republic of Washington" and "Federal Republic of America," the Convention named the new country the Confederate States of America.

Over the years, considerable confusion in the historical record has been created by the existence of both a provisional and a permanent government. For example, Jefferson Davis was inaugurated President twice: first as the President of the provisional government that existed from February 8, 1861 to February 18, 1862; and a second time as President of the government established by the Constitution of the Confederate States of America as the permanent government which began to function on February 18, 1862.

The Provisional Congress was the legislature of the provisional government and was unicameral. Under the permanent government, the Congress was bicameral, as in the United States, with a Senate and a House of Representatives. The Congresses of the permanent government were numbered, the number changing every two years with the election of a new House of Representatives, just as is done in the United States. For this reason, we say that the United States Congress which was elected in 1986 was the One Hundredth Congress, and the First Congress of the United States was elected in 1788.

In the Confederate States there were two numbered Congresses. The First Congress was elected in 1861 and served from February 1862 until February 1864. The Second Congress was elected in 1863 and served from February 1864 until the destruction of the government in 1865. If, therefore, in our discussion of Confederate flag laws, we mention the "Provisional Congress," the reference is to the Congress of the temporary government in

1861; if to the "First" or "Second Congress," the reference is to one of the Congresses of the permanent government from 1862 to 1865.

The Confederate Flag is properly the official flag of the Confederate States; i.e., the national flag. Often people will use the term "Confederate Flag" to describe one of the flags used by the army as a battle flag. In the course of this book the term "Confederate Flag" will only be used in reference to the national flags of the Confederate States of America.

The discussion of flags will of necessity use some vexillological terms which may not be familiar to you. "Vexillology" is a rather difficult word to pronounce, and sounds like some great technical field of science. As it is derived from the Latin word "vexillum," meaning flag, the suffix "ology" meaning "The study of," the word "vexillology" means quite simply the study of flags. In order to help the reader understand these terms, a glossary is provided here.

GLOSSARY OF VEXILLOLOGICAL TERMS

BORDER: An edging to a flag which is of a different color than the field of the flag and is used for either decorative purposes or to prevent fraying.

CANTON: This is also known as the union of the flag. It refers to the upper left-hand corner of the flag.

ENSIGN: The national flag as used on a ship.

FIMBRATION: A narrow edging, often white, used to separate different colored features on a flag. The rules of heraldry prohibit the placing of color upon color.

FLY: The length of the flag.

FLY END or FLY EDGE: The width of the flag at the point farthest from the staff.

HOIST: The width of the flag at the point nearest the staff.

JACK: A small flag designating nationality and flown at the bow of a naval vessel while in port.

FLAGS OF THE CONFEDERACY

MULLETT: An heraldic device said to have originally represented the rowel of a spur, more often referred to now as a star. It is most often shown with five points, although more are used at times.

SAINT GEORGE'S CROSS: An upright cross in "+" form, this feature was derived from the flag of England.

SALTIER or SALTIRE: A cross traversing a flag from corner to corner in "x" form. Also referred to as a Saint Andrew's cross, this feature was derived from the flag of Scotland.

PART I—THE NATION

CHAPTER 2
"STARS AND BARS"

Adoption

For the first twenty-four days of the existence of their government, the Confederate States of America had no officially approved flag. When Jefferson Davis was inaugurated President of the provisional government on February 18, 1861 the capitol building in Montgomery flew the flag of the State of Alabama, and the inaugural parade was lead by a company of infantry carrying the flag of Georgia.

The Provisional Congress had established a Committee on Flag and Seal, the chairman of which was William Porcher Miles of South Carolina. The Committee received hundreds of designs for flags which were submitted to it by citizens from all parts of the country. Even citizens of States still among the United States sent in proposals. An unwritten deadline for the adoption of a flag was March 4, 1861 because on that date Abraham Lincoln was to be inaugurated president of the now foreign United States; and on that date the Southern States were determined to fly a flag which expressed their own sovereignty.

As the deadline neared, the Committee continued to examine and debate designs without being able to reach a consensus. The patterns submitted could be divided generally into two categories: those which bore some resemblance to the flag of the United States and flags of intricate and complex design. The Committee, and especially Chairman Miles, discredited all those imitating the United States' flag as being too easily confused with the flag of the old union. A sentimental attachment to "the old flag" felt by the public at large, however, made it impossible to ignore the elements of its design. The category of intricate designs was ruled out as being too difficult and expensive to render into bunting flags. The Committee finally had to admit its inability to agree on a flag and chose four patterns to present to the full Congress for a final decision.

On the morning of March 4, large cambric models of the proposed flags were hung up on the walls of the Congressional chamber. The models of the three rejected patterns did not survive the War, but we are able to reconstruct them from a description given by Chairman Miles in an 1872 letter to General P.G.T. Beauregard.

The first of these three is now a familiar design: a blue saltier fimbrated in white on a red field, with white stars upon the saltier. This flag was designed by Chairman Miles, whose inspiration may have been the banner

FLAGS OF THE CONFEDERACY

Figure 1: Proposed Flag of the Confederate States,
Submitted to Congress March 4, 1861 by William Porcher Miles.

of the South Carolina Secession Convention. The Convention flag had been red with a blue Saint George's cross which bore fifteen stars representing the slaveholding States. Its canton featured the crescent and palmetto of the State. The Congress rejected Miles' flag: one member even ridiculed it as resembling "a pair of suspenders." The difficulty of achieving a symmetrical arrangement of the seven stars (one for each of the seven Confederate States in March 1861) on the arms of the cross may have prejudiced Congress' consideration of this proposal.

Miles' flag would not die, however, and in various alterations went on to become the battle flag of the Confederate armies. Before the end of the War, Miles' "pair of suspenders" would be incorporated into the flag of the Confederate States and, as the canton of the ensign of the CSS *Shenandoah*, would circumnavigate the globe.

The other proposals rejected by the Confederate Congress were never to be seen again. One of these was closely patterned on the flag of the United States. Its blue union displayed a star for each of the Confederate States, but the stripes were changed from red and white to red and blue. Mr. Miles could not remember, in 1872, how many stripes were on the model. Probably there were seven to represent the original Confederate States in keeping with the precedent of thirteen stripes to represent the thirteen original United States.

The third flag rejected by Congress bore no resemblance to the flag of the United States. It was described by Chairman Miles as "a red field with a blue ring or circle in the center." Presumably the ring is representative of the solidarity of the Southern States, but there is no statement of its symbolism in Miles' 1872 letter to Beauregard.

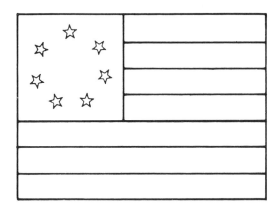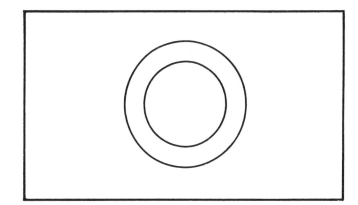

Figures 2-3: Two of the Flags Submitted to the
Provisional Congress on March 4, 1861.

The flag which received the blessing of Congress was described in the following language:

> The flag of the Confederate States of America shall consist of a red field with a white space extending horizontally through the center, and equal in width to one-third the width of the flag. The red space above and below to be the same width as the white. The union blue extending down through the white space and stopping at the lower red space. In the center of the union a circle of white stars corresponding in number with the States in the Confederacy.

The text of this description was inserted into a report of the Committee on Flag and Seal which may have already been prepared save for the description of the flag. The report was then written into the journal of the Congress.

Arrangements had already been made for a flag-raising ceremony to be held on the afternoon of March 4; but a flag had just that day been decided upon. "Thanks to fair and nimble fingers," however, to quote Chairman Miles from his 1872 letter again, a flag made of merino was completed within two hours of its adoption. This very first flag of the Confederate States of America was hoisted over the capitol building in Montgomery by Miss Letitia Christian Tyler, the granddaughter of President John Tyler.

In their hurry to adopt the flag and have it prepared for the ceremony to be held that afternoon, Congress neglected to formally enact a flag law. The journal of the Congress reflects the report of the Committee on Flag and Seal, but indicates nothing with regard to a vote. Nor do the statute books of the Confederate States contain a Flag Act of 1861. Despite official use for over two years, the "Stars and Bars" was never established as the Confederate Flag by the laws of the land.

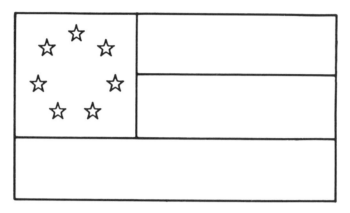

Figure 4: Flag of the Confederate States of America,
Adopted by the Provisional Congress, March 4, 1861.

The use of this new flag not only spread rapidly across the Confederate States but also among Confederate sympathizers in States still in the old Union. Six weeks later, it was flying over Fort Sumter in Charleston harbor as a flag of a nation at war. With war came alterations in the flag because, by the third week in May, Virginia and Arkansas had been admitted to the Confederacy adding two more stars to the flag. The circle grew to eleven with the addition of North Carolina and Tennessee in July. Missouri in November and Kentucky in December brought to the flag a new constellation of thirteen stars. In this final form, the "Stars and Bars" would see official use until its replacement in 1863.

Designer

In the first half of the Twentieth Century, a great controversy erupted over the origin of the design of the first flag of the Confederate States. The claimants to the honor were Nicola Marschall, a Prussian artist who lived in Montgomery, Alabama and Orren Randolph Smith of North Carolina. Both men claimed to have submitted to the Provisional Congress the design destined to later become famous as the "Stars and Bars." Mr. Marschall also claimed to have submitted two other unsuccessful patterns.

The controversy between Marschall and Smith seems to have arisen about 1911, but it was not until 1915 that it was officially investigated. At

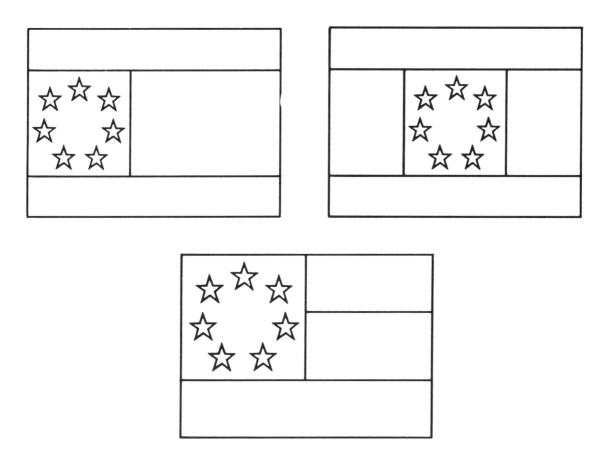

Figures 5-7: Three Flag Designs Submitted to the
Provisional Congress by Nicola Marschall.

that time the Stars and Bars Committee of the United Confederate Veterans at their Richmond reunion held during June 1-3 of 1915 found in favor of Mr. Smith's claim, as evidenced by the published report of the committee. The debate continued, however, and in 1931 the Alabama Department of Archives and History published the results of an investigation by the Alabama legislature which determined that Mr. Marschall had in fact designed the flag.

Both sides produced convincing evidence as well as contradictions during these investigations. Contradictions should always be expected when attempting to reconstruct from memory events which have transpired more than fifty years earlier. However a recently discovered letter dated March 2, 1861 seems definitely to establish Marschall's claim. Given simplicity of the design and the early enthusiasm for the flag bearing some resemblance to that of the United States, it is possible that Mr. Smith also submitted a very similar proposal. The evidence presented to the United Confederate Veterans and the Alabama legislature may well entitle both men to claim the honor of being "Father of the Stars and Bars."

Specifications

The report of the Committee on Flag and Seal established some, but not a complete set of, specifications for the relative proportions of the elements of the "Stars and Bars." The canton or union was to be equal in width to two-thirds the width of the flag. Each bar was to be equal to one-third the width of the flag. No direction was given as to the length of the canton or the overall length of the flag.

An exhaustive survey of surviving Confederate Flags done by Howard Michael Madaus of the Milwaukee Public Museum and reported in the monograph *"Rebel Flags Afloat"* (*Flag Bulletin,* No. 115, Vol. XXV, Nos. 1-2, January-April 1986) found that by far the largest number of first national pattern flags had cantons which were square, or nearly so.

Only about a quarter of the flags studied had cantons which were definitely rectangular; on some the width exceeded the length, and on others the length exceeded the width.

There was no definite pattern with regard to length. Over 70 percent of the "Stars and Bars" flags in the Madaus survey fell into the rather broad category of having lengths between one and one-half and two times their widths.

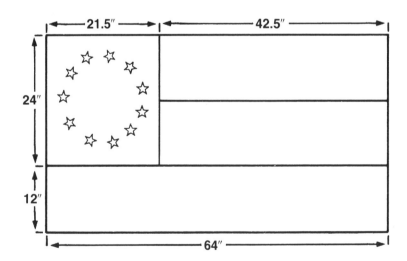

Figure 8: Specifications of a Representative Example
of the "Stars and Bars."

STARS AND BARS

The flag shown in the illustration is a representative example but should by no means be taken as definitive of proportions. The Committee report left a lot of room for interpretation.

The illustrated flag has eleven stars in the canton and would have been official from the time Tennessee was admitted to the Confederacy on July 2, 1861 until the admission of Missouri on November 28 of that year. Kentucky was admitted as one of the Confederate States on the following December 10, and the thirteen-star flag was official from that date until the "Stars and Bars" was replaced as the Confederate Flag on May 1, 1863.

CHAPTER 3
"STAINLESS BANNER"

Towards A More Confederate Flag

William Porcher Miles was not satisfied with the "Stars and Bars." He did not share in the sentimental attachment to the old flag and wished the adoption of a new symbol which could not in any way be thought similar to that of the United States. To his chagrin, his desires were not reflected in the mood of the people or of their representatives in Congress in 1861.

As the War extended from weeks into months, the sentimental feelings felt for the "Stars and Stripes" began to wane. More and more Confederate citizens came to see what one member of Congress referred to as "the old gridiron" as the symbol of oppression and imperialistic aggression. In February, 1862 the First Congress of the Confederate States assembled in Richmond. Its recently elected membership reflected the changing attitudes of the people towards the flag.

Among the first actions of the new Senate and House of Representatives was the appointment of a Joint Committee on Flag and Seal with instructions to consider and propose a new Confederate Flag. On April 19, 1862 the Joint Committee submitted its report to both Houses of Congress. The report, introduced in the form of a joint resolution, read as follows:

A JOINT RESOLUTION adopting the flag of the Confederate States of America

Resolved by the Congress of the Confederate States of America, That the flag of the Confederate States shall be as follows: A red field, charged with a white saltier, having in the centre the device of a sun, in its glory, on an azure ground, the rays of the sun corresponding with the number of the States composing the Confederacy.

In its report on the flag, the Committee stated that the azure (blue) ground on which the sun was charged would be in the form of a shield. The symbolism of the flag was described in these words:

The red field denotes nautical powers, boldness, courage, valour.

The saltier, an "honourable ordinary" in heraldry, is the emblem of progress and strength; its white indicating purity, innocence, and gentleness.

The blue of the shield represents justice and faith, perseverance and vigilance.

The sun manifests the dominion, generosity and stability of the Confederacy.

Nearly all the designs submitted to the committee contained a combination of stars. This heraldic emblem, however, has been descended as a manifestation of our entire and absolute severance from the United States at the complete annihilation of every sentiment indicating the fainted hopes of reconstruction.

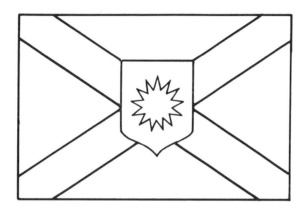

Figure 9: Flag Proposal of the Joint Committee on Flag and Seal—April 19, 1862.

The Senate designated the resolution Senate Resolution No. 11, but took no vote while the House of Representatives began immediate debate on the resolution. Congressman Miles expressed his approval of the design, saying that he was "glad that a flag had been adopted [by the committee] so dissimilar to the old."

Some members of the House of Representatives received the Committee's flag proposal favorably and urged immediate adoption. Others resisted the proposal. Representative Charles M. Conrad of Louisiana's second congressional district did not consider the flag attractive and expressed concern that, since it had no canton, the Committee's design could not be inverted as a signal of distress at sea. The observation by Mr. Miles that the flags of most maritime nations had no cantons did not impress the Louisianian.

A number of members of the House of Representatives wanted to put off consideration of the flag. Some were more inclined to adopt a Confederate flag that more nearly resembled the battle flag used by the army in Virginia. Others were concerned about the lack of a consensus in favor of the

FLAGS OF THE CONFEDERACY

Committee's flag. April 19, 1862 would not see the birth of a new Confederate flag. The House of Representatives voted 39 to 21 to postpone consideration of the resolution. It was never again brought up for discussion in the halls of Congress.

The change would be made in 1863. On April 22 of that year, the Committee on Flag and Seal of the Confederate States Senate reported a bill which was designated Senate Bill No. 132. It read as follows:

AN ACT to establish the flag of the Confederate States.
The Congress of the Confederate States of America do enact, That the flag of the Confederate States shall be as follows: a white field with the battle flag for a union, which shall be square and occupy two thirds of the width of the flag, and a blue bar, one third of the flag in its width, dividing the field lengthwise.

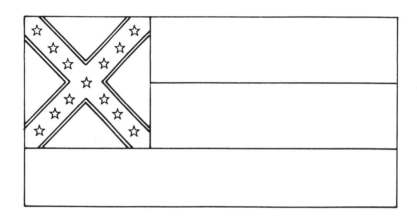

Figure 10: Original Version of the Flag in Senate Bill No. 132, 1863.

The bill was passed by the Senate on the same day and sent to the House of Representatives.

The flag which this bill proposed sought to cure the similarity between the "Stars and Bars" and the "Stars and Stripes" by reversing the colors of the former. Rather than a blue union and bars of red, white and red, the new Confederate flag proposed by the Senate would have a red union with bars of white, blue and white. The red battle flag of the Army of Northern Virginia would provide the canton of this new flag.

Although Senate Bill No. 132 passed the Senate with little debate and on a voice vote on the day that it was reported out of committee, it would not receive such easy approval in the House of Representatives. The House was much more radical on the flag issue than the Senate. The Representatives demanded even less resemblance to the Northern flag than that which had been approved in Senate Bill No. 132.

Figure 11: A Proposed Amendment of Senate Bill No. 132, 1863.

The House of Representatives took up the debate on May 1, 1863. Motions were immediately made to effect various amendments to the bill. The first successful motion removed the bars altogether and replaced them with a white field bordered in red, with the battle flag still in canton. The canton itself was reduced in size by another motion from two-thirds to three-fifths the width of the flag. Congressman Ethelbert Barksdale of Mississippi made a motion to remove the stars from the cross. He believed that "the flags of the two countries [should be] as distinct as the character of the two people." The majority of the House did not wish to go as far as the Mississippian, and the stars stayed.

Figure 12: Congressman Swan's Proposed Amendment to Senate Bill No. 132.

FLAGS OF THE CONFEDERACY

William G. Swan of Tennessee's second congressional district wished to substitute the following language:

> That the flag of the Confederate States shall be as follows: A red field with a Saint Andrew's cross of blue edged with white and emblazoned with stars.

Swan, who before secession had been mayor of Knoxville and attorney general of Tennessee, had adapted his proposal from the battle flag of the Army of Northern Virginia, but it was in fact identical to the flag proposed by William Porcher Miles in March 1861. But in the intervening years, the battle flag had been sanctified by the blood of Southern soldiers in the struggle for independence. Swan wished to adopt it for use by the nation now as a tribute to the valor of the Confederate fighting man.

William Porcher Miles rose to speak on the subject. He was quite proud that the flag which he had designed and urged upon Congress in 1861 had been adopted by the military with such success. In recording Representative Miles' address, the Minutes of the Third Session of the First Congress (*Southern Historical Society Papers*, Volume 49, p. 272) outlined his argument:

> The country was aware how it had been received by the army—it had been consecrated. The battle flag should be used then with simplicity, but to the demand that it should be taken alone, he would reply that it was necessary to emblazon it. The battle flag, on a pure white field, he thought was the best they could find. The white flag could be easily distinguished, and would not be taken as a flag of truce—it was the old French Bourbon flag. They should abandon the border—it was unusual. It was not intended to follow strictly the requirements of heraldic art, but some attention should be paid to good taste. He trusted that the battle flag on a pure white field, discarding the blue bar and border (a monstrosity), would be adopted.

Robert P. Trippe of Georgia's seventh congressional district urged postponing consideration of a new flag. This was the last day of the session and he believed that it was precipitous to be "deciding on the flag of a great nation in fifty-five minutes, what remains of the actual session." Congress would not be put off, though time would give the appearance of prophesy to Congressman Trippe's words.

"STAINLESS BANNER"

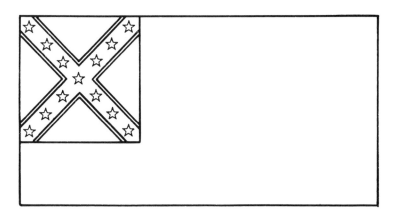

Figure 13: Flag of the Confederate States of America,
May 1, 1863 to March 4, 1865.

Finally, Representative Peter W. Gray of Houston, Texas put into formal language an amendment to Senate Bill No. 132 which read as follows:

AN ACT to establish the flag of the Confederate States.
The Congress of the Confederate States of America do enact, That the flag of the Confederate States shall be as follows: The field to be white, the length double the width of the flag, with the union (now used as the battle flag) to be a square of two-thirds the width of the flag, having the ground red; thereon a broad saltier of blue, bordered with white, and emblazoned with white mullets or five-pointed stars, corresponding in number to that of the Confederate States.

In this form Senate Bill No. 132 passed the House of Representatives and was returned to the Senate for concurrence in the amendment. The Senate approved the amendment with little or no debate. Later that afternoon President Davis' signature gave a new national flag to the Confederate States of America.

This second Confederate Flag was referred to as the "Stainless Banner" because of its pure white field, and was proclaimed emblematic of the purity of the Cause which it represented. Regrettably, one of its first uses was to drape the coffin of General Thomas J. "Stonewall" Jackson. On the evening of May 2, 1863 General Jackson was fired upon by one of his own regiments at the Battle of Chancellorsville. His left arm was amputated, and his health seemed to improve until May 7, by which time he had developed pneumonia. On May 10, the hero of the Southern nation was dead and on May 12, his body lay in state in the Confederate House of Representatives chamber. His coffin, by order of the President, was draped with the first of the new national flag to be manufactured. This very first "Stainless Banner" is now on display in the Museum of the Confederacy in Richmond.

Figure 14: Confederate States Treasury Note Decorated
with the Confederate Flag and a Portrait of Stonewall Jackson.

Because the first use of the new Confederate flag was connected with Jackson's funeral, it is at times referred to as the "Jackson flag." This identification of the flag with Jackson would be strengthened by the use of the Stainless Banner and Jackson's portrait together on Confederate bonds and currency issued in 1864 and 1865.

Specifications

The Flag Act of 1863 gives a bit more detail on relative proportions than did the report adopting the "Stars and Bars." When combined with further details set out in regulations issued by the Secretary of the Navy on May 26, 1863 for the construction of the naval ensign, full and complete specifications are available for almost every detail of the flag.

The Flag Act of 1863 specified that the length of the flag was to be twice its width. For example, a 54 inch wide flag would have a length of 108 inches. The canton of this 108 inch long flag would be a 36 inch square. The proportions of the cross and stars are not provided in the act, but they are set out in some detail in the naval regulations. The arms of the cross were to be proportioned in width as 1/4.8 the width of the canton; i.e., seven and one-half inches in our example. The white border of the cross of our flag will be one and three-fifths inches wide at a specified size of 1/22 the width of the canton. Finally, the stars are to have a diameter of 1/6.4 the width of the canton, or about five and one-half inches on our example. Using the Flag Act of 1863 in combination with the naval regulations, it is quite possible to construct in accurate detail the official dimensions of the "Stainless Banner."

During the War these detailed specifications were not very strictly followed. A large number of the surviving flags have lengths much less than twice their widths. In a number of cases, the canton is rectangular rather than square. Very little effort seems to have been made to measure the stars to their regulation sizes.

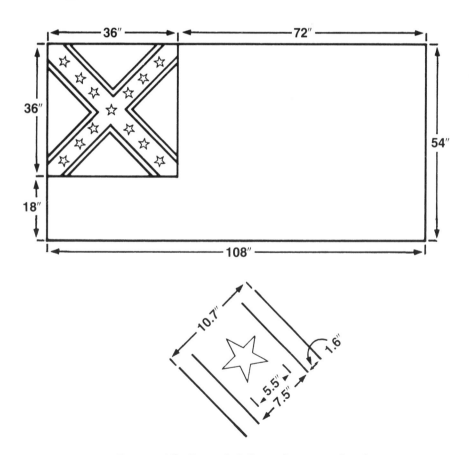

Figure 15: Detailed Specifications for the
Construction of the Stainless Banner.

CHAPTER 4
THE CONFEDERATE FLAG — FINAL EDITION

Revision Of The "Stainless Banner"

The Flag Act of 1863 solved the problem of clear national identity and a complete vexillological separation from the United States, but the new flag would present new problems. Congressman Miles had argued in the 1863 flag debate that "the white flag . . . would not be taken for a flag of truce—it was the old French Bourbon flag"; but the flag had been considered by many as looking too much like a flag of truce. As a result, the flag was often manufactured with a shorter fly length in order to minimize the white field.

To address this problem, a new flag bill was introduced in the Confederate States Senate on December 13, 1864. Senator Thomas J. Semmes of Louisiana introduced Senate Bill No. 137 with the statement that "naval officers objected to the present flag—that in a calm it looked like a flag of truce." The text of the bill was as follows:

AN ACT to establish the flag of the Confederate States.
The Congress of the Confederate States of America do enact, That the flag of the Confederate States of America shall be as follows: The width two-thirds of its length, with the union (now used as the battle flag) to be in width three-fifths of the width of the flag, and so proportioned as to leave the length of the field on the side of the union twice the width of the field below it; to have the ground red and a broad blue saltier thereon, bordered with white and emblazoned with mullets or five-pointed stars, corresponding in number to that of the Confederate States; the field to be white, except the outer half from the union to be a red bar extending the width of the flag.

Senate Bill No. 137 was referred to the Naval Committee on December 13. Senator Albert G. Brown of Mississippi read the Committee's report, which included a recommendation for passage, to the Senate on December 16. This time, however, the Congress would not pass a flag law without a great deal of consideration. Senator Edward Sparrow of Louisiana recommended that opinion of officers of the army should be obtained on the matter. Senator Semmes replied that he had received a letter from "the most distinguished officer" of the army (General Lee?) expressing the opinion that the officers of the navy were the proper parties to resolve the flag question. Nevertheless, in an abundance of caution, the Senate referred the bill to the Military Committee.

The Military Committee considered the bill for seven weeks and made its report recommending passage without amendment on February 5, 1865. The Senate passed Senate Bill No. 137 on February 6 and sent it on to the House of Representatives.

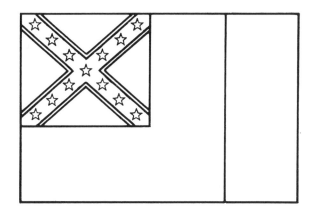

Figure 16: Flag of the Confederate States of America
Since March 4, 1865.

On February 7 the new flag bill was referred to the House Committee on Flag and Seal. That committee kept the bill for twenty days and also reported favorably on it. The House passed Senate Bill No. 137 on February 27. On March 4, 1865, President Jefferson Davis signed the bill into law, and the Confederate States of America acquired their third and last national flag. The Flag Act of 1865 became law exactly four years after the Provisional Congress had adopted the "Stars and Bars" as the first Confederate Flag.

Specifications

The Flag Act of 1865 made fairly detailed changes in the proportions of the flag, as well as in its general appearance. In addition to adding the broad red bar to the fly end, it shortened the fly length of the flag and changed the canton from a square to a rectangular shape.

The 1865 law specifies that the width of the flag shall be two-thirds its length. In the case of a flag 60 inches wide, the proper length would be 90 inches. The canton of a 60 inch wide flag at a specified width of three-fifths that of the flag will be 36 inches wide. The law specifies that the canton will be so proportioned as to leave the length of the field beyond it "twice the width of the field below it." On a 60 inch wide flag, this will leave a canton length of 42 inches, thus creating a width to length ratio for the canton of 6/7.

The red bar on our illustrated flag would be 24 inches wide at a specified width of one-half the area of the fly beyond the canton.

It seems proper to apply the navy regulations of 1863 to this new flag for a determination of the cross and star proportions. Since our 60 inch flag under the 1865 law has the same canton width as the 54 inch wide flag under the 1863 law, the cross and star proportions on the two flags would be the same: a seven and one-half inch wide cross with a one and three-fifths inch wide border and stars with a five and one-half inch diameter.

Unlike the existing War period flags of the earlier patterns, there are very few survivors of the 1865 version. Of the ones which do exist, most are the 1863 flag with the fly shortened and a red bar added.

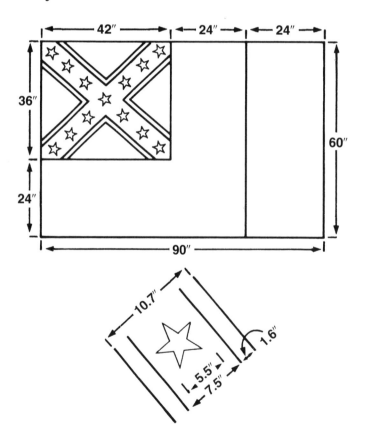

Figure 17: Detailed Specifications for the
Construction of the Last Confederate Flag.

CHAPTER 5
EVOLUTION OF THE FLAG

While it may not be immediately apparent, the national flag of the Confederate States of America has evolved by a direct and traceable lineage from the flag of the United Kingdom of Great Britain.

In 1606, King James VI of Scotland, also known as King James I of England, established a new flag for the United Kingdoms of England and Scotland. The king combined the Saint George's flag of England with the Saint Andrew's flag of Scotland to form the Union flag of Great Britain. At sea, this Union flag was placed as a canton hence also called a union, on a red flag to become known as the "British red ensign." Because of the maritime nature of American colonization, it was this red ensign which became best known in British America.

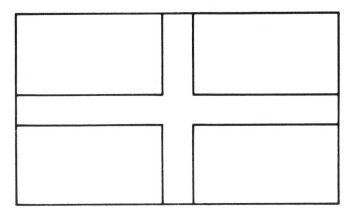

Figure 18: St. George's Cross of England

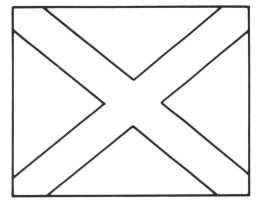

Figure 19: St. Andrew's Cross of Scotland

FLAGS OF THE CONFEDERACY

Figure 20: Union Flag
of Great Britain 1606-1801.

Figure 21: British Red Ensign
Prior to 1801.

When the Revolution broke out in 1775, the Americans adopted various banners to display their political sentiments. Among those often appeared the British red ensign charged with some motto such as "LIBERTY." In December 1775, John Paul Jones hoisted upon an American ship a red ensign which had been altered by the addition of white stripes, creating thirteen red and white stripes to represent the rebel colonies. A similar flag was raised in the American lines outside of Boston by General George Washington just after the turn of the new year in 1776. This striped ensign, which was called the Grand Union Flag, came to be accepted as the common flag of the united colonies. With the Declaration of Independence on July 4, 1776 it became the first national flag of the United States of America and served that role until June 14, 1777.

In June, 1777, the Continental Congress decided that the flag should be altered by removing from the blue union the crosses of England and Scotland. In their stead were placed the stars of the American States, and thus was born the "Stars and Stripes." Over time new States were admitted to the American union, which in turn were represented by new stars in the union of the flag. Custom came to prefer five-pointed stars, though stars with more points would be used until the middle of the nineteenth century.

In 1861, when the Southern States left the American union and formed the new Confederacy, they chose for the new nation a flag with the same elements as the old, but reduced the thirteen stripes to three bars. As in the case of the Continental Congress in 1777, by 1863 the Confederate Congress was ready to remove from their flag reminders of the old government. An initial proposal to reverse the colors of the "Stars and Bars" was amended by removing the bars altogether, leaving the red battle flag of the army as a canton on a "stainless" white field.

Figure 22: Flag of the United States—1776 to 1777

In 1865, with concern expressed by naval officers that the flag of 1863 could be mistaken for a flag of truce, the dimensions were altered and a red bar was added to the fly creating the last flag of the Confederate States of America.

Figure 23: Flag of the United States—1777 to 1795

FLAGS OF THE CONFEDERACY

Thus was established the long and proud heritage of the Confederate Flag. One could say that the British Union flag, in the form of the red ensign, was the great-great-great grandfather of the Confederate Flag of 1865. In the tradition of biblical genealogy, we could fashion a geneaology of the Confederate Flag as follows:

The Union flag of 1606 and its red ensign begat the Grand Union flag of 1775, the symbol of American liberty;

the Grand Union flag begat the "Stars and Stripes" of 1777, the symbol of American independence;

the "Stars and Stripes" begat the "Stars and Bars" of 1861, the symbol of Southern liberty;

the "Stars and Bars" begat the "Stainless Banner" of 1863, the symbol of Southern independence; and

the "Stainless Banner" begat the Confederate Flag of 1865, the final expression in bunting of the sovereignty of the Confederate States of America.

PART II—THE STATES

CHAPTER 6
THE BONNIE BLUE FLAG

On January 9, 1861, the Convention of the People of Mississippi adopted an Ordinance of Secession. With the announcement of the Ordinance, a large blue flag bearing a single white star was raised over the capitol building in Jackson. One of the witnesses to this event, an Irish-born actor named Harry Macarthy, was so inspired by the spectacle that he wrote a song entitled "The Bonnie Blue Flag" which was destined to be the second most popular patriotic song in the Confederacy. (See Appendix D)

The first recorded use of a lone star flag dates to 1810. At that time the portion of Louisiana east of the Mississippi River, along with the southern portions of Mississippi and Alabama, made up the Spanish province of West Florida. This area had once been part of the French province of Louisiana. In 1763, after the French and Indian War, France ceded New Orleans and all of Louisiana west of the Mississippi to Spain. That portion of Louisiana east of the river was ceded to the English, who established therein the British province named West Florida. West Florida was conquered by Spain during her campaigns as an American ally in the Revolutionary War. When France later re-acquired Louisiana from Spain, there was a dispute about whether or not the transaction included West Florida. Spain refused to relinquish control of the province, and the United States inherited the dispute when they purchased Louisiana from France in 1803.

The inhabitants of West Florida were in large part English-speaking people on whom the authoritarian rule of Spain did not wear well. They were disappointed in the failure of the United States to annex the territory, and in 1804 an unsuccessful revolt was lead by the brothers Reuben, Nathan, and Sam Kemper. In the years following the Kemper Rebellion, the English-speaking people of West Florida attempted to secure some degree of traditional English liberties within the framework of their Spanish government. This culminated in a convention of the people meeting in 1810 to press for some form of constitutional guarantees. Governor de Lassus pretended to cooperate with the convention while sending to the Governor of East Florida for troops to put down this perceived threat to his authority.

Upon learning of the Governor's duplicity, the supporters of the convention turned to open rebellion. On Saturday, September 11, 1810, a troop of dragoons under the command of Major Isaac Johnson set out for the provincial capitol at Baton Rouge. At the head of the column rode a color sergeant carrying a blue flag with a single, white five-pointed star. This flag had been made a few days before by Mrs. Melissa Johnson. Together with other republican forces under the command of Colonel Philemon Thomas, these men captured Baton Rouge without loss to themselves, imprisoned the Governor, and on September 23, 1810 raised their Bonnie Blue flag over the Fort of Baton Rouge. Three days later, John Rhea, president of the West Florida Convention, signed a Declaration of Independence, and the lone star flag became the emblem of a new republic.

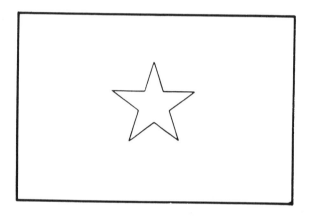

Figure 24: The Bonnie Blue Flag.
- Flag of the Republic of West Florida September 16 to December 10, 1810.
- Flag of the Republic of Texas, December 10, 1836 to January 25, 1839.
- Flag of the Republic of Mississippi January 6 to January 26, 1861.

The Republic of West Florida was short-lived. When Spanish rule was removed from the country with neither the use of American troops nor risk to itself, the government of the United States was interested in asserting its claim to the little republic. On October 27, 1810, President Madison issued a proclamation declaring West Florida under the jurisdiction of the Governor of the Louisiana Territory. On December 10, the flag of the United States replaced the Bonnie Blue flag over Baton Rouge, and The Republic of West Florida passed into history.

The memory of the West Florida movement lived on in Southern tradition, and the flag of the little nation became the flag of the Republic of Texas from 1836 to 1839. It would rise again as the unofficial flag of the Republic of Mississippi for a few weeks in 1861; and Harry Macarthy's song would spur it on into the romantic lore of the South. When the song was first played in New Orleans before a mixed audience of Texans and Louisianians, it was received with an outburst of approval that was nearly riotous. Thereafter, the Bonnie Blue flag spread across the nation and into the hearts of the people. Although the Confederate government did not adopt it, the Confederate people did, and lone star flags were adopted in one form or another in five of the southern States which adopted new flags in 1861.

CHAPTER 7
STATE FLAGS

The secession movement saw the first large-scale use of flags by the American States. After the Revolution, most of the States retired their revolutionary colors and displayed only the flag of the Union. With the resumption of their independence, the Southern States adopted new banners to reflect their new status among the States of the earth. Of the Confederate States which had adopted official State flags by the end of 1861, only one had a flag in use before she seceded from the Union. Three of those States—Virginia, South Carolina, and, of course, Texas—still fly the flags which were flown in 1861.

South Carolina

South Carolina was the first State to leave the United States and was among the first to adopt a new national flag. The design chosen was drawn from South Carolina's revolutionary heritage.

The crescent had been the symbol of South Carolina in the days of the colonial government. During the Revolution, South Carolina troops wore silver crescents as hat badges and fought under blue flags with a white crescent in the upper corner. The other emblem of South Carolina is the palmetto tree. Its use also dates from the Revolution and is said to have been inspired by the palmetto logs used in the construction of Fort Moultrie

Figure 25: Flag of South Carolina,
January 26, 1861 to January 28, 1861.

34

on Charleston harbor. Because palmetto is resilient, the logs absorbed the shock from British cannon balls instead of shattering under them; they are credited with contributing to the successful defense of Charleston on June 28, 1776. Shortly after this battle, the palmetto was adopted as the central device of the Great Seal of South Carolina.

Figure 26: Flag of South Carolina,
January 28, 1861 to Present.

Prior to secession, South Carolina patriots had often displayed palmetto flags. Secession saw these multiply, with each flag-maker designing the flag according to her own fancy. On January 26, 1861 the legislature adopted an official flag which embraced both of the State's historic devices. The new emblem was the old revolutionary flag with the white crescent. Added to the center of the field was a large white oval on which appeared a palmetto tree in natural colors. Two days later the legislature altered the flag by removing the oval and placing a white palmetto tree on the blue field. In this final form, the palmetto flag has served South Carolina to the present.

Mississippi

On January 9, 1861, Mississippi became the second State to secede from the United States. To celebrate her new role as an independent republic, the Bonnie Blue flag was freed to the wind from the flagpole of the State capitol in Jackson.

Mississippi adopted an official State flag on January 26, 1861. Her new flag incorporated the Bonnie Blue flag as a canton on a white field. In the center of the field was a representation of a magnolia tree in natural colors,

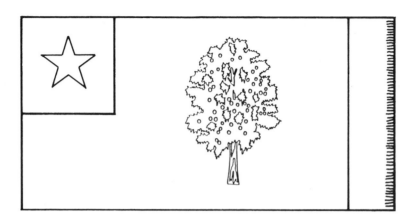

Figure 27: Flag of Mississippi Adopted January 26, 1861.

an association so permanent that the State is still known as the Magnolia State. The fly end of the magnolia flag was decorated with a red fringe.

Florida

Florida withdrew "from the confederacy of States existing under the name of the United States of America" by the adoption of her Ordinance of Secession on January 10, 1861. Some time passed before she acquired an official State flag, in part because the legislature was unable to agree on a design. On February 8, 1861 a law was enacted delegating to the governor the power to designate a flag.

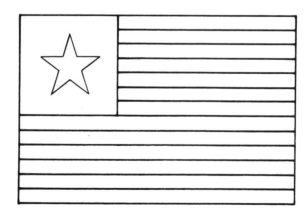

Figure 28: Provisional Flag of Florida, January 13, 1861 to September 13, 1861.

STATE FLAGS

In the meantime, the Military Department of the State adopted a provisional flag to be used until the governor provided a State flag. This provisional flag was promulgated by an order dated January 13, 1861 and was simply the flag of the United States with a single star in the union.

Figure 29: Flag of Florida Adopted September 13, 1861.

The Governor finally issued an executive order establishing the State flag on September 13, 1861. The flag adopted by the Confederate Congress on March 4, 1861 was altered to serve Florida's needs by extending the canton to form a vertical bar the entire width of the flag. Centered on the blue bar was a new seal for the State, displaying in natural colors a stand of arms and flags beneath an oak tree, with ships at sea in the background.

Alabama

In anticipation of the secession of Alabama, some ladies of Montgomery painted a beautiful flag for presentation to the State. The Alabama Convention approved the flag and, upon the adoption of the Ordinance of Secession, the new Alabama flag was raised over the capitol of the independent republic.

Alabama's banner was unique among Southern State flags in being two-sided; that is, the front and back had different designs. The central device on the front of the blue flag was the goddess Liberty dressed in red with a sword in her right hand and a Bonnie Blue flag in her left. This Bonnie Blue flag was edged in yellow and had a yellow star. Above the star in yellow letters was the name "ALABAMA." Also in yellow letters and arched over the goddess was the legend "INDEPENDENT NOW AND FOREVER."

Figure 30: Flag of Alabama.

The reverse of the flag was also a field of blue. Featured on the reverse was a cotton plant guarded by a rattlesnake, below which appeared the Latin motto "NOLI ME TANGERE." The motto translates "Don't Touch Me" and together with the snake was reminiscent of the "Don't Tread On Me" flags of the Revolution.

Figure 31: Reverse of the Alabama State Flag.

Attractive as this flag was, it was not easy to make, and Alabamians apparently borrowed one of its details to serve as a simpler flag. This was the Bonnie Blue flag with the yellow star held by the Liberty on the official standard. It may have appeared at times with the word "ALABAMA" over the star, but the most common form seems to have been with the yellow star alone on the blue field.

STATE FLAGS

Georgia

On the day that Georgia's Convention adopted "An Ordinance to dissolve the union between the State of Georgia and other States united with her under the compact of government entitled 'The Constitution of the United States of America,' " a new flag was raised over the capitol in Milledgeville. This flag has been described as the arms of Georgia on a white field. The arms feature the arch of the Constitution being supported by the pillars of Justice, Wisdom, and Moderation.

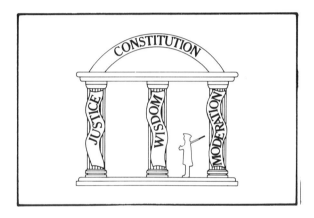

Figure 32: The Flag of Georgia.

Over the years, tradition has placed this device more often on a blue field, and it may have been used on a blue field as a military color. Georgia's State flags in this century have continued the tradition of displaying the State seal on blue. A surviving Georgia flag in the collection of the Museum of the Confederacy in Richmond, however, places the arms on a red field.

Georgia's flag had a position of honor on the occasion of Jefferson Davis' inauguration as President of the provisional government. On February 18, 1861 the Confederate States did not yet have a flag, and the President-elect's inaugural parade was led by a company of re-coated Georgia militia marching under the flag of the State of Georgia.

Louisiana

The pelican has been the symbol of Louisiana for almost as long as there has been such a place. The bird which now graces the flag of the State has been the device of the Seal of Louisiana since its territorial status under the United States. While the current flag has only been official since 1912,

Figure 33: Pelican Flag.

pelican flags are known to have existed before the War Between the States. One such flag was used at the Louisiana Secession Convention on the occasion of the adoption of the Ordinance of Secession on January 26, 1861.

When she adopted an official flag to proclaim her independence after secession, Louisiana turned away from the pelican. Instead, she chose a flag

Figure 34: Flag of Louisiana, Adopted
February 11, 1861.

which combined the sentimental attachment she felt for the United States flag with the lone star symbol of sovereignty and colors from her heraldic past.

Like the flag of the old Union, the new flag adopted by Louisiana on February 11, 1861 had thirteen stripes. These were altered from the red and white of the United States to the blue, white and red of France, Louisiana's mother country. The canton of the flag placed a single yellow star on a field of red, the colors of the flag of Spain which had also once held dominion over Louisiana.

Texas

Texas had the richest vexillological heritage of any American State. The flags of six independent powers have flown over her territory. During the period which Texans consider to have been their glory—the era of the Republic--six flags flew to represent Texan nationalism.

Figure 35: Flag of the Texas Revolution, 1835.

When the Texas Revolution began in 1835, the predominant sentiment was not for independence, but for liberty under the law, as established by the Mexican Constitution of 1824. The flag of the Revolution proclaimed this, and Texas was represented by the flag of Mexico, the green-white-red tri-color, with the national arms replaced by the date "1824."

The response of Santa Anna to the demands of the Texans left little room for reconciliation, and by 1836 the revolution had become a secession movement. On March 2, 1836 the independence of Texas was proclaimed, and

FLAGS OF THE CONFEDERACY

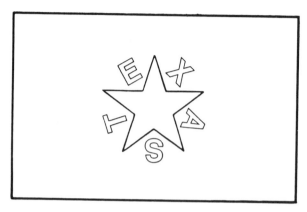

Figure 36: Texas Flag, March 11, 1836
to December 10, 1836.

on March 11 the Republic adopted a new flag devoid of Mexican symbolism. This standard was the Bonnie Blue flag with letters spelling out the name "TEXAS" arrayed around and between the points of the star. On December 10, 1836, the flag was modified by removing the letters, and the unadorned Bonnie Blue flag of the late Republic of West Florida with a yellow star served as the national flag of Texas for the next two years.

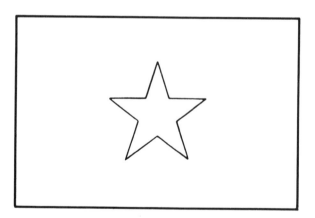

Figure: 37: Texas Flag, December 10, 1836 to January 25, 1839; and unofficial variant of the Alabama State Flag, 1861.

On January 25, 1839 the Republic of Texas made a final modification of its flag. The blue field was reduced to a vertical bar, its width approximately one half the width of the flag, but still carrying the lone star of the Republic. The remainder of the flag became two broad bars of white over red. This flag has served Texas ever since: first as the flag of the Republic until 1845; then as the flag of the State under the United States; and finally as the flag of the State under the Confederate States of America.

During the era of the Republic, Texas also had distinctive flags for use at sea. During the pre-independence period of the revolution, Texas privateers

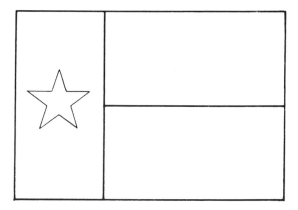

Figure 38: Texas Flag, January 25, 1839 to Present.

flew the "1824" flag. In 1836, this was replaced by the ensign of the Texas Navy. The Texas naval ensign proclaimed the attachment of Texas to the United States, both symbolically and diplomatically, and was in fact the flag of the United States with a lone star in the union. This ensign graced the naval vessels of the Republic until Texas became one of the United States in 1845.

During the time the Bonnie Blue flag served as the national flag of Texas,

Figure 39: Texas Naval Ensign.

it probably also served as the national ensign for private and merchant ships belonging to Texans. With the adoption of the new national flag in 1839, a new and distinctive civil ensign was also adopted by the Congress of Texas. The civil ensign rearranged the features of the national flag to form a horizontal tri-color with bars of white, blue and red. The lone star was displayed in the center of the blue bar, which was twice as wide as the white

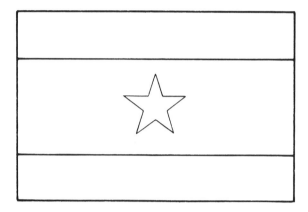

Figure 40: Texas Civil Ensign.

or red bars. Although the civil ensign ceased to be used after Texas joined the American union in 1845, the Flag Law of 1839 does not appear to have been amended. It would still be appropriate for Texans who wished to fly a Texas flag from their boats or ships to display the civil ensign of 1839. Texas is therefore one of the few American States to have a distinctive civil ensign.

Virginia

On April 15, 1861 Lincoln's Secretary of War called upon Virginia to supply regiments for the invasion and conquest of the Confederate States. The Old Dominion responded by withdrawing from the United States on the 17th of April; and on the 30th of that month, a flag was adopted for the independent Commonwealth of Virginia.

Virginia's banner is the Bonnie Blue flag with the star replaced by the seal of the Commonwealth. The seal, which had been adopted during the Revolution, represents the goddess Liberty striking down an allegorical tyrant, his crown dashed to the earth. Both the seal and flag display the Latin

Figure 41: Virginia State Flag.

motto "SIC SEMPER TYRANNIS": which translates as "Ever Thus to Tyrants." The symbol which had been adopted as Virginia's response to monarchial and parliamentary tyranny in the 1770s would serve as her reply to aggression in the 1860s. In slightly modified form, the flag of 1861 still serves the Commonwealth of Virginia.

North Carolina

On May 20, 1861 exactly eighty-six years after North Carolina is said to have expressed her determination for independence from Great Britain in the Mecklenburg Resolves, the people of North Carolina assembled in convention once again declared their independent spirit and removed themselves from the jurisdiction of the United States government. On June 22, 1861 North Carolina adopted a flag which commemorated both of these events.

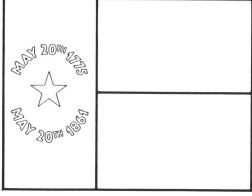

Figure 42: North Carolina State Flag.

FLAGS OF THE CONFEDERACY

The North Carolina State flag followed the lone star theme which had been adopted in Alabama, Florida, Louisiana, Mississippi and Texas. The Old North State was inspired by the flag of Texas in choosing a pattern, but the Carolinians reversed the colors. Carolina's star was placed on a broad red vertical bar from which flowed horizontal bars of blue over white. Around the star were placed the dates on which North Carolina celebrates her independence: May 20, 1775 for independence from Great Britain and May 20, 1861 for independence from the United States.

Tennessee

On April 25, 1861 the Tennessee General Assembly convened in Nashville in the second extraordinary session of the legislature to be called since the turn of the year. The first extra session had put to a vote of the people the question of joining the deep South in seceding from the Union. Taking a wait-and-see attitude towards the Lincoln government, the people rejected secession in the February election; but in April, war had become a reality, and the questions was again to be placed before the voters.

On the first day of the session, the speaker of the Senate, Tazewell B. Newman, offered Senate Resolution No. 2 to establish a flag for the State of Tennessee. The resolution called for the Secretary of State to have a flag of the Confederate States made which would be modified by replacing the stars with the Great Seal of Tennessee. Senate Resolution No. 2 was referred to the Committee on Federal Relations, but was never acted upon further and never became a law. The committee thought it impolitic to fly an obviously Confederate flag while Tennessee was still one of the United States.

Figure 43: Proposed Tennessee State Flag, 1861.

STATE FLAGS

Despite the inaction of the Tennessee legislature, the flag recommended by Senator Newman did see some limited use. At least two Tennessee infantry regiments used "Stars and Bars" style flags with the Tennessee State seal painted in the canton. A modern version of Newman's flag is used by Tennessee descendants of Confederate soldiers. At its 1983 convention, the Tennessee Division of the Sons of Confederate Veterans adopted as its official flag the "Stars and Bars," with the stars replaced by the original version of the State seal as adopted in 1801 and used from 1802 to 1829.

Kentucky

Kentucky was the last State to leave the old Union and become one of the Confederate States, and in this action she was divided. Her State legislature remained loyal to the United States; but a convention of her people meeting at Russellville on November 18-20, 1861, declared Kentucky to be independent of the United States, deposed the State government, and established a provisional government. Under the auspices of the provisional government, Kentucky was admitted to membership in the Confederate States of America.

Figure 44: The Seal of the State of Kentucky.

FLAGS OF THE CONFEDERACY

No State flag was ever officially adopted by the provisional government of Kentucky. On January 16, 1862 the council of the provisional government did pass legislation creating a new State seal. The act described the new seal as:

> an arm with a star in the hand offering it to a constellation of twelve stars, with the word "Kentucky" above and "Voce Populi" beneath.

The seal was kept in the custody of the Secretary of State of the provisional government, but its post-war fate is unknown. Although some have been tempted to speculate on the existence of a Kentucky flag using this seal on the center of a blue field, there is, at this time, no evidence of the existence of such a flag.

Arkansas and Missouri

Neither Arkansas nor Missouri enacted legislation to adopt an official State flag. A flag was adopted in Missouri by direction of General Sterling Price, commander of the Missouri State Guard. When orders were issued in the Spring of 1861 for district commanders of the State Guard to prepare their troops for active duty, they were instructed that each regiment was to carry a Missouri flag, which was to be made of blue merino with the State arms in gold on both sides.

Figure 45: Flag of Missouri

PART III—MILITARY AND NAVAL FLAGS

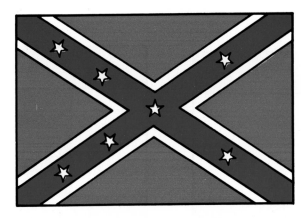

Figure 1: Proposed Flag of the Confederate
States, Submitted to Congress March 4,
1861 by William Porcher Miles.

 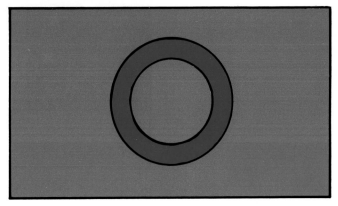

Figures 2-3: Two of the Flags Submitted to the Provisional Congress on March 4, 1861.

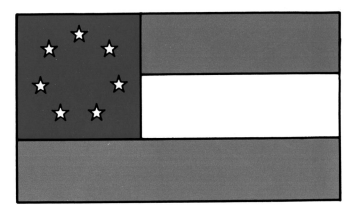

Figure 4: Flag of the Confederate States of America,
Adopted by the Provisional Congress, March 4, 1861.

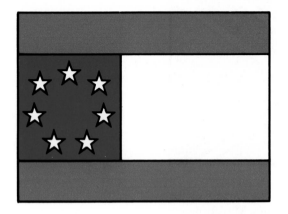
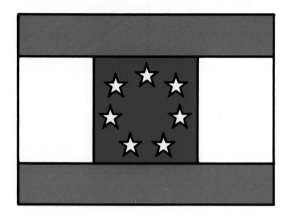

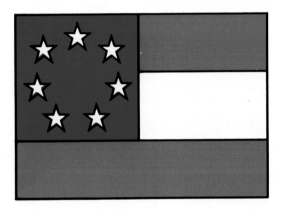

Figures 5-7: Three Flag Designs Submitted
to the Provisional Congress by Nicola Marschall.

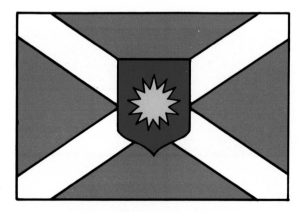

Figure 9: Flag Proposal of the Joint Committee
on Flag and Seal—April 19, 1862.

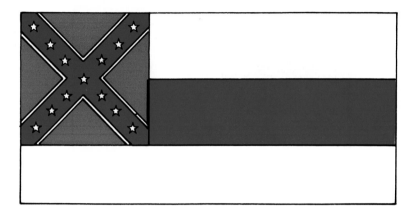

Figure 10: Original Version of the Flag in Senate Bill
No. 132, 1863.

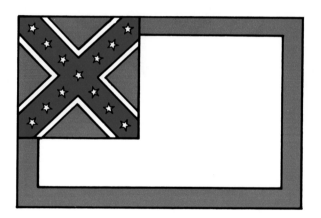

Figure 11: A Proposed Amendment of
Senate Bill No. 132, 1863.

Figure 12: Congressman Swan's Amendment to Senate Bill No. 132.

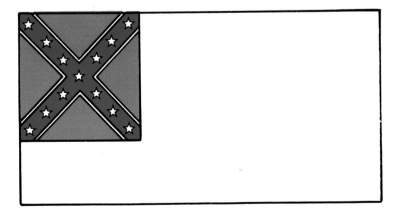

Figure 13: Flag of the Confederate States of America,
May 1, 1863 to March 4, 1865.

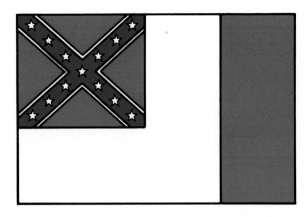

Figure 16: Flag of the Confederate States of America Since March 4, 1865.

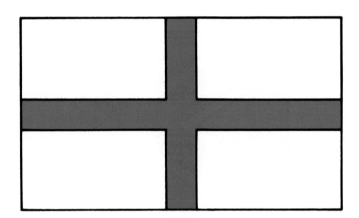

Figure 18: St George's Cross of England.

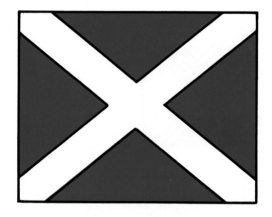

Figure 19: St. Andrew's Cross of Scotland.

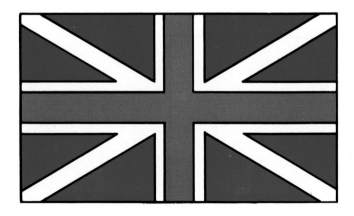

Figure 20: Union Flag of Great Britain 1606-1801.

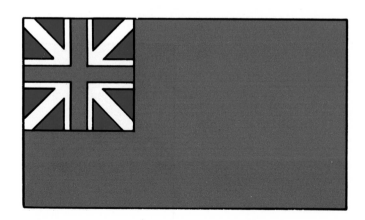

Figure 21: British Red Ensign Prior to 1801.

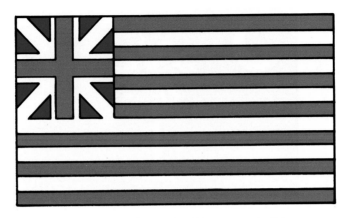

Figure 22: Flag of the United States—1776 to 1777.

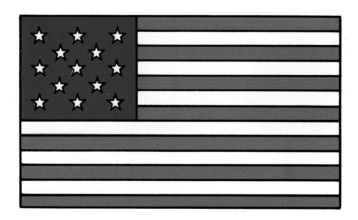

Figure 23: Flag of the United States—1777 to 1779.

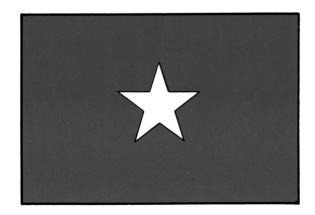

Figure 24: The Bonnie Blue Flag.

Figure 25: Flag of South Carolina, January 26, 1861 to January 28, 1861.

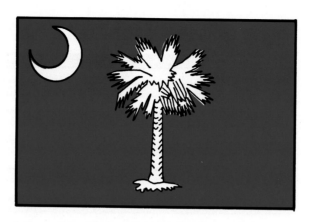

Figure 26: Flag of South Carolina, January 28, 1861 to Present.

Figure 27: Flag of Mississippi, Adopted January 26, 1861.

Figure 28: Provisional Flag of Florida, January 13, 1861 to September 13, 1861.

Figure 29: Flag of Florida, Adopted September 13, 1861.

Figure 30: Flag of Alabama.

Figure 31: Reverse of the Alabama State Flag.

Figure 32: The Flag of Georgia.

Figure 33: Pelican Flag.

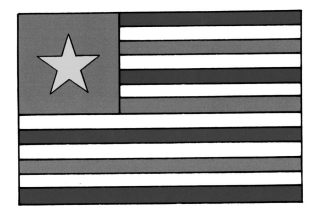

Figure 34: Flag of Louisiana, Adopted February 11, 1861.

Figure 35: Flag of the Texas Revolution, 1835.

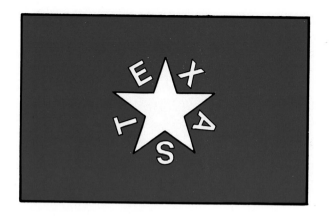

Figure 36: Texas Flag, March 11, 1836 to December 10, 1836.

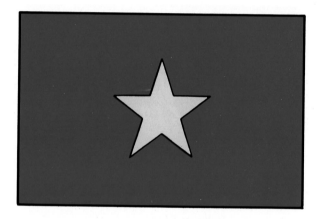

Figure 37: Texas Flag, December 10, 1836 to January 25, 1839; and Unofficial Variant of the Alabama State Flag, 1861.

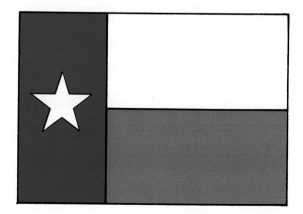

Figure 38: Texas Flag, January 25, 1839 to Present.

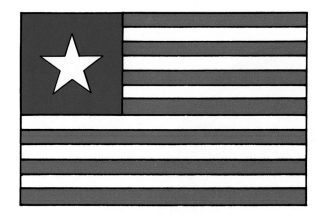

Figure 39: Texas Naval Ensign.

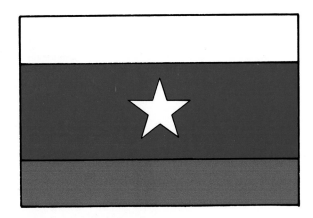

Figure 40: Texas Civil Ensign.

Figure 41: Virginia State Flag.

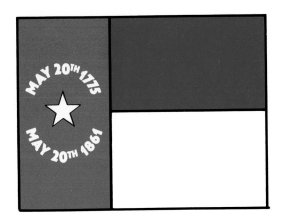

Figure 42: North Carolina State Flag.

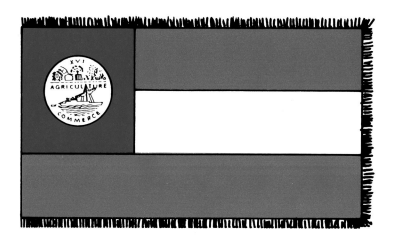

Figure 43: Proposed Tennessee State Flag, 1861.

Figure 44: The Seal of the State of Kentucky.

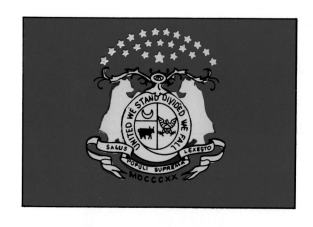

Figure 45: Flag of Missouri.

Figure 46: General Beauregard's Prototype of the Battle Flag.

Figure 47: Silk Battle Flag, Issued November 1861.

Figure 48: First Bunting Issue, 1862.

Figure 49: Third Bunting Issue, 1863, Army of Northern Virginia.

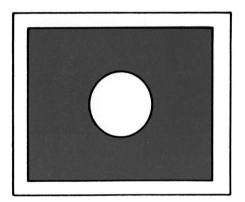

Figure 50: Hardee's Corps, Army of Tennessee.

Figure 51: Polk's Corps Battle Flag, Army of Tennessee.

Figure 52: Bragg's Corps Battle Flag,
Army of Mississippi, First Pattern.

Figure 53: Bragg's Corps Battle Flag, Army
of Mississippi, Second Pattern.

Figure 54: Army of Tennessee Battle Flag,
1864.

Figure 55: Battle Flag of the Department
of South Carolina, Georgia and Florida.

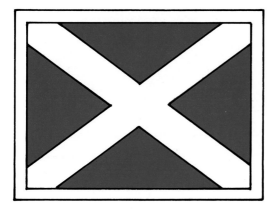

Figure 56: Battle Flag of the Department of East Tennessee.

Figure 57: Battle Flag of the Department of Alabama, Mississipi, and East Louisana.

Figure 58: Battle Flag of Shelby's Division.

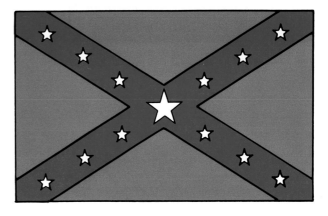

Figure 59: Battle Flag of Parson's Texas Cavalry.

Figure 60: Battle Flag of General Richard
Taylor's Army.

Figure 61: Trans-Mississippi Department, Van Dorn's Corps.

Figure 62: Trans-Mississippi Department, The "Missouri Battle Flag."

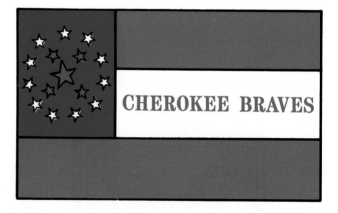

Figure 63: Trans-Mississippi Department,
Cherokee Nation.

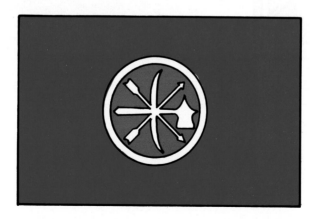

Figure 64: Flag of the Choctaw Brigade.

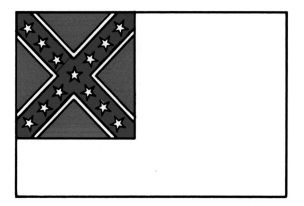

Figure 66: Confederate States Naval Ensign After May 26, 1863.

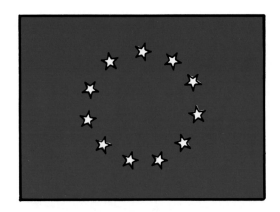

Figure 67: Confederate Navy Jack March 4, 1861 to May 26, 1863.

Figure 68: Confederate Navy Jack After May 26, 1863.

Figure 69: Confederate Commission Pennant, March 4, 1861 to May 26, 1863.

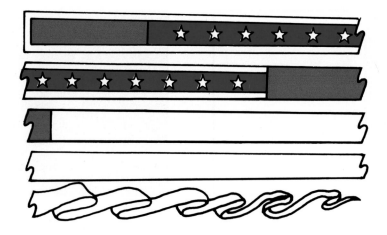

Figure 70: Confederate Commission Pennant,
After May 26, 1863.

Figure 71: Variant Confederate Commission Pennant,
Used After May 1, 1863.

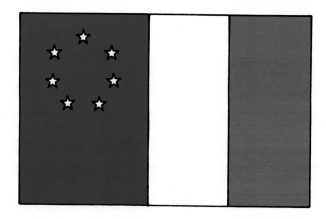

Figure 72: Confederate States Revenue Service
Ensign.

CHAPTER 8
BATTLE FLAGS

The use of distinctive battle flags by units of the army is not unique to the Confederacy. For centuries British regiments have carried, in addition to the King's Colors, a distinctive regimental flag. From the War of 1812 through the War Between the States, infantry regiments of the United States carried a blue battle flag emblazoned with the eagle and shield of the Union.

In the Confederate States, there were a number of battle flags used by the army. Those used in the Eastern theatre, where the army tended to get more support from the government, were fairly uniform. The armies in the Western theatre and Trans-Mississippi, more remote from the government in distance and attention, had greater diversity in the styles and patterns of battle flags. Uniformity of flags among the Western troops was never truly achieved and only approached realization in the last year of the War.

The Army of Northern Virginia

The Confederate Army in Virginia was always considered the grand army of the South. Called the Army of the Potomac while under the leadership of General Joseph E. Johnston in 1861 and early 1862, it gained immortality under the command of General Robert E. Lee as the Army of Northern Virginia. Its legendary position in history was guaranteed by the greatness of its commander and by the pre-eminence placed upon it by the government in Richmond.

The first great battle of the army was the Battle of Manassas fought on July 21, 1861. Nominally commanded by General Johnston, the greatest part of the planning and actual field operations were handled by General P.G.T. Beauregard, the "hero of Fort Sumter." On numerous occasions during the course of the battle, confusion was caused by the inability of commanders to distinguish their troops from those of the enemy. There was no distinct uniform for either army at this time, both sides having units clothed in grey and blue along with other more exotic and spectacular colors. The heat and dust of battle combined to obscure visibility. Added to these difficulties was the fact that the "Stars and Bars" were so similar to the "Stars and Stripes" that many men in both armies believed the other side had used the flag of his opponent as a *ruse de guerre*. Time would remedy the uniform confusion; the obscurity caused by battle smoke and

51

dust could never be eliminated; but Beauregard was determined to remedy the flag problem at once.

General Johnston sought initially to solve the problem by having the troops use their State flags, but only the Virginia regiments were sufficiently supplied to accomplish this. General Beauregard contacted Congressman William Porcher Miles to attempt to have the Confederate flag changed. Miles was sympathetic, but informed the General that Congress would not agree to a change. Miles suggested that the army address the issue by adopting for its own use a distinctive battle flag and recommended the design which he had urged upon the Congress as the Confederate Flag on March 4, 1861.

Figure 46: General Beauregard's Prototype of the Battle Flag.

Beauregard liked the red flag with its blue cross and stars. Johnston liked it too, but recommended that it would be more convenient for military use if made square. Three prototypes were made by Hettie, Jennie, and Constance Cary and presented to Generals Johnston, Beauregard and Earl Van Dorn. Johnston approved the issuance of these battle flags in September 1861 and ordered the quartermaster of the army to have flags made up in silk and distributed to the regiments. By tradition, the silk for these flags was dress material donated by the ladies of Virginia. November 1861 would see the first issue to the army of the flag to become known as the "Southern Cross." On the crosses were twelve stars for the eleven States then in the Confederate States, and Missouri, which had seceded but was not yet admitted as a member of the Confederacy. The outer edges were bordered in yellow, and the flag was attached to its staff by a dark blue sleeve.

52

BATTLE FLAGS

Figure 47: Silk Battle Flag,
Issued November 1861.

The heavy campaigning of the army was hard on these silk flags, requiring a new issue to be made in 1862. The replacement battle flags were made of a high quality English wool bunting, designed to last and wear well. All subsequent issues of battle flags to the Army of Northern Virginia would be made of wool bunting.

Figure 48: First Bunting Issue, 1862.

The first two issues of bunting flags differed from their silk predecessors in several design details. The number of Confederate States had increased to thirteen, and all subsequent battle flags issued in Virginia would have a thirteenth star at the junction of the cross. The yellow border on the outer edges was replaced by an orange border, and the sleeve was replaced by a white canvas heading with eyelets through which cord could pass to attach the flag to its staff. Under these flags, Lee's army would fight such great battles as Cedar Mountain, Sharpsburg, and Chancellorsville.

Figure 49: Third Bunting Issue, 1863, Army of Northern Virginia.

After the Battle of Chancellorsville and before the army left Virginia for the invasion of the United States which would culminate in the Battle of Gettysburg, a third issue of bunting flags was made to the army of Northern Virginia. The only major change at this time was the replacement of the orange border with one of white. This is the form which would later become the most familiar version of the "Southern Cross" and would eventually be identified by many as the only proper Confederate battle flag. The flags of this issue often have the regimental designation painted in gold on the blue cross above and below the central star. The regiment's battle honors were painted in blue on the red field of the battle flag.

Under this final form of the Army of Northern Virginia battle flag, Lee fought the battles of Gettysburg, the Wilderness, Cold Harbor, Petersburg, and countless others before the end at Appomatox Court House. The battle flag in Virginia was issued in different sizes for the different services: 48 inches square for the infantry, 36 inches for the artillery, and 30 inches for the cavalry.

The Army Of Tennessee

In February 1862 General Beauregard was transferred to the Western theatre of operations, where the Confederate army was under the command of General Albert Sidney Johnston. Beauregard played the role of a dominant second-in-command to this Johnston, as he had to Joseph E.

BATTLE FLAGS

Johnston in Virginia, and he endeavored to have the battle flag of the army in Virginia issued to the Western regiments.

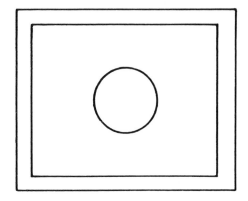

Figure 50: Hardee's Corps, Army of Tennessee.

The great stumbling block to the "Southern Cross" in the West was the fact that some of the army corps commanders had already adopted and issued their own distinctive battle flags to avoid the confusion caused by the "Stars and Bars." One such design was issued to the regiments commanded by General William J. Hardee, author of the light infantry manual used by the armies of both countries during the War. Hardee's flag was blue, with a white border and a central white disk, sometimes referred to as a "silver moon." This disk would vary in shape from round to oval, and at times was almost a square with rounded corners. Regiments would often paint their unit designation on the white disk and their battle honors on the blue field or the border.

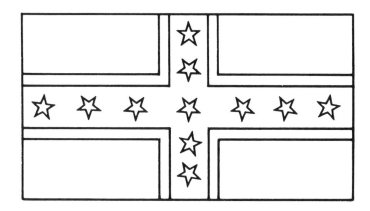

Figure 51: Polk's Corps Battle Flag, Army of Tennessee

FLAGS OF THE CONFEDERACY

Another corps which had adopted its own battle flag was that of Major General Leonidas Polk. His standard, like Beauregard's, had as its major feature a cross adorned with stars. Polk, however, appears to have been influenced by his non-military vocation in the design of his flag. In addition to his role as a Confederate general, Polk was the Episcopal Bishop of Louisiana. The emblem of the Episcopal Church is the red cross of Saint George, the national emblem of England, and this cross became the central device of Polk's battle flag. The red cross was separated from the blue field of the flag by a white fimbration and carried white stars on its arms to represent the States in the Confederacy.

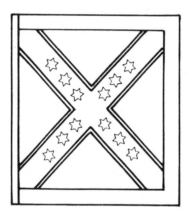

Figure 52: Bragg's Corps Battle Flag,
Army of the Mississippi, First Pattern.

When General Braxton Bragg's corps was added to the army in February 1862 its regiments had no distinctive battle flag. Beauregard took advantage of this lack by having flags of the "Southern Cross" pattern made for these troops. Bragg's new battle flags corresponded closely to those issued in Virginia in November 1861. They were made of wool bunting instead of silk, and the twelve stars had six points. This first Western version of the "Southern Cross" was bound on its outer edges by a broad pink border.

After the first shipment of these flags was received, Beauregard apparently ordered another set to be issued as needed in the future. This second set was of the same material and construction as the first, but the pink border was on all four sides of the flags, which were made oblong instead of square.

The remaining corps of the Confederate Army of the Mississippi was the reserve corps commanded by General John C. Breckinridge of Kentucky, the former Vice President of the United States. Breckinridge's regiments continued to use the "Stars and Bars" national flag of the Confederate States.

Thus were set the basic patterns used by the Army of the Mississippi when it gathered to meet the enemy near Shiloh Church; a distinctive battle flag for each of the main army corps and the national flag for the reserve corps. The multiplicity of flags continued through 1862, in November of which the army was re-named the Army of Tennessee, and only increased after Congress adopted a new Confederate national flag in 1863. [Note: The main Confederate army in the Western theatre was called the "Army of the Mississippi" from March 5, 1862 to November 20, 1862. See, *Official Records of the Union and Confederate Armies in the War of the Rebellion*, Series I, Volume 10, Part I, pp. 596-7, and Volume 16, pp. 886.]

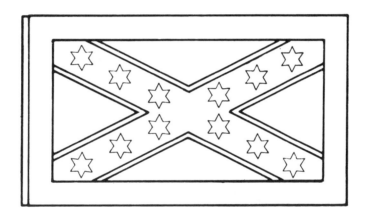

Figure 53: Bragg's Corps Battle flag,
Army of the Mississippi, Second Pattern.

On December 18, 1864, following Braxton Bragg's disastrous defeat at Chattanooga, command of the Army of Tennessee was transferred to General Joseph E. Johnston. Johnston's first goal was to restore the morale and *esprit d'corps* of the army. One of the ways by which he effected this revitalization was by the issuance of new and uniform battle flags to his regiments during the months of March and April 1864.

The Army of Tennessee battle flag was of the "Southern Cross" pattern and differed from its Virginia parent mainly in being rectangular instead of square. The Army of Tennessee flag had average dimensions of 36 inches in width by 52 inches in length. Those issued to artillery batteries were about 30 inches wide and 42 inches long. They had thirteen stars and no border.

General Johnston's flag did not achieve uniformity for the Army of Tennessee. The regiments of General Patrick Cleburne's division reacted so strongly to the ordered change of flags that they were allowed to keep their old Hardee pattern banners, though new flags of this pattern were issued to them. The flag of the Army of Tennessee is now the most commonly encountered form of the "Southern Cross," and the flag sold at souvenir stands throughout the South.

Figure 54: Army of Tennessee Battle Flag, 1864.

The Department Of South Carolina, Georgia And Florida

In addition to their field armies, the Confederate States were divided into a number of geographical military departments. Troops within those departments were based at permanent forts, camps and stations and used for the defense of their departments.

The Department of South Carolina, Georgia, and Florida was one of the

Figure 55: Battle Flag of the Department
of South Carolina, Georgia and Florida

first military departments created during the war effort. While its boundaries changed at times, for the most part it encompassed all of South Carolina along with tidewater Georgia and eastern Florida. In the first year of the war, the regiments in that department primarily used their State flags. In September, 1862, General Beauregard assumed command of the department and replaced the State flags with the "Southern Cross."

The battle flag of this department was very similar to that used in Virginia after the middle of 1863. It was a square bunting flag with a white border and thirteen five-pointed stars. The main difference between the flags was that the stars of the battle flag of the Army of Northern Virginia were grouped towards the junction of the cross, leaving the outer reaches of the arms unoccupied, while the stars of the department's flags were evenly spaced on the arms of the cross. Also, unlike the Virginia battle flags, which were tied to their staffs through several eyelets, the battle flags of the Department of South Carolina, Georgia, and Florida were attached by means of a sleeve sewn to the heading of the flag.

The flags of this department were issued in different sizes for the different branches of the service, as were those in Virginia. Service branch was also indicated by the color of the pole sleeve with blue for infantry and red for artillery.

Department of East Tennessee

The Department of East Tennessee was under the command of General Edmund Kirby Smith in 1862. During Bragg's Kentucky campaign, Kirby Smith's troops left their department and were called the Army of Kentucky. There is evidence that during this time the regiments of the Department of East Tennessee carried a distinctive battle flag.

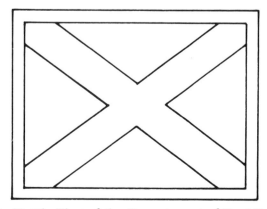

Figure 56: Battle Flag of the Department of East Tennessee.

FLAGS OF THE CONFEDERACY

The East Tennessee battle flags were apparently the traditional Saint Andrew's Cross of Scotland: an unadorned white saltier on a blue field. Borders and edgings on these flags seem to have varied, and there is no uniformity of size or construction among those which survive.

Department Of Alabama, Mississippi, and East Louisiana

The Department of Alabama, Mississippi, and East Louisiana existed in 1864 and 1865. It covered all of Alabama, Mississippi, and that portion of Louisiana which lies to the east of the Mississippi River.

Figure 57: Battle Flag of the Department of
Alabama, Mississippi, and East Louisiana.

Battle flags used by the regiments of this department were regularly issued and were manufactured in Mobile, Alabama, from a standard pattern. Generally following the "Southern Cross" flag of the Army of Tennessee, this battle flag was unbordered, made of wool bunting, and made with the leading edge folded over to form a pole sleeve. The white stars were equally spaced on the arms of the fimbrated blue cross. Instead of the thirteen stars found on the flags of the Army of Tennessee, however, the battle flags of this department omitted the star at the junction of the cross. This seems to be characteristic of flags made in Mobile. Even second national pattern Confederate Flags manufactured in this area omitted the thirteenth star.

The department's battle flag was generally 45 inches wide and about 52 inches long. A smaller version, measuring 37 inches in width by 46 inches in length, was issued to the regiments of Lieutenant General Nathan Bedford Forrest's cavalry corps.

The Trans-Mississippi Department

The Trans-Mississippi Department was geographically the largest military department in the Confederate States. It was composed of all of Louisiana west of the Mississippi River, the entire States of Arkansas, Missouri and Texas, the Indian nations in what is now Oklahoma, and the Confederate Territory of Arizona which included the southern portions of modern Arizona and New Mexico. After the fall of Vicksburg in July, 1863, the Department was isolated from the rest of the Confederate States and in large measure operated independently of the authorities in Richmond in military matters. It was also the last part of the Confederate States to fall to the Yankee invasion. At the beginning of 1865, Texas was almost entirely free of Northern soldiers.

Figure 58: Battle Flag of Shelby's Brigade.

The Trans-Mississippi was unique among Confederate military departments in that its military forces were significantly bi-racial. In 1861 the Confederate States entered into nine treaties with the Indian nations and tribes in the area now known as the State of Oklahoma. The treaties with those Indians known as the "civilized nations" — the Cherokee, Chickasaw, Choctaw, Creek, and Seminole — included mutual defense provisions under which an estimated three thousand Indian soldiers served in the Confederate army. These soldiers fought valiantly and provided valuable service in the Trans-Mississippi Department. The last Confederate general to surrender his command was Stand Watie of the Cherokee Nation, and the last Confederate civil authorities to submit to the invaders were Governor Winchester Colbert and the Council of the Chickasaw Nation.

Several incarnations of the "Southern Cross" battle flag were used in the Trans-Mississippi Department. One very close to that used by the Army of Northern Virginia was a surviving flag from General Jo Shelby's Missouri Brigade. The silk flag was bordered in white, as were the later issue battle flags in Virginia, and added to the white border on three sides is a red silk fringe. It is fortunate that this flag survives. General Shelby did not surrender his division at the end of the War. With two hundred volunteers who did not wish to be reconstructed, he rode across Texas for Mexico. On July 4, 1865 Shelby had his survivors weight their battle flags with stones and sink them in the Rio Grande before they crossed into Coahuila. One of Shelby's men rescued this flag from its watery grave before crossing over.

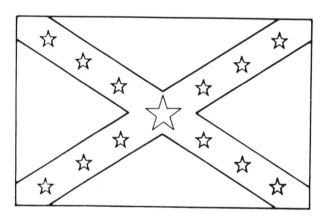

Figure 59: Battle Flag of Parson's Texas Cavalry.

Other far western troops used flags of the "Southern Cross" pattern more nearly resembling those of the Army of Tennessee. Flags such as the one used by Parson's Texas Cavalry Brigade were borderless and oblong. They also tended to violate the rules of heraldry by omitting the white edging of the cross. Another feature often found on flags from the Trans-Mississippi, especially those associated with Texas, was that the central star was larger than the other stars of the cross.

In March 1864 the forces of General Richard Taylor defeated their Northern opponents and re-established Confederate control over western Louisiana. The battle flags under which these men fought were also patterned on the "Southern Cross," but these had the colors reversed, with red crosses on

BATTLE FLAGS

Figure 60: Battle Flag of General Richard Taylor's Army.

blue grounds.   Like other flags in this Department, the cross was not separated from the field by a white edging.   At least one of Taylor's regiments, the First Arkansas Cavalry, used a variant with a Saint George's Cross similar to those used by the regiments of General Leonidas Polk in Tennessee in 1862.

Figure 61: Trans-Mississippi Department,
Van Dorn's Corps.

A number of Trans-Mississippi commands used more singular standards.   One such was the flag of Earl Van Dorn's Army of the West.   The Van Dorn battle flag had a red field adorned with thirteen white stars arranged in five rows, with a white crescent in the upper corner.   The flags were bordered in yellow or white.   When General Van Dorn brought his regiments to the east side of the river in 1862 to join Beauregard's army at Corinth, Mississippi, they brought these flags with them and fought under them at the Battle of Corinth in October of that year.

Figure 62: Trans-Mississippi Department,
The "Missouri Battle Flag".

Another distinctively Trans-Mississippi flag was associated almost exclusively with Missouri regiments in that Department, resulting in its identification as the Missouri battle flag. The blue flag was bordered in red on its outer edges. A white Roman cross adorned the field near the hoist of the flag.

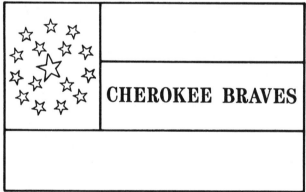

Figure 63: Trans-Mississippi Department,
Cherokee Nation.

When Confederate Indian Commissioner Albert Pike signed the treaty with the Cherokee Nation on October 7, 1861, he presented to Principal Chief John Ross a special flag. This "Stars and Bars" Confederate flag had added within its circle of white stars a cluster of five red stars to represent the five "civilized nations" of Indians with whom the Confederate States had a special relationship. A similar flag survives which was credited to the First Cherokee Mounted Rifles and suggests that this design may have had unofficial use as a national flag by Confederate Cherokees.

BATTLE FLAGS

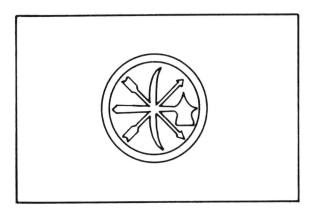

Figure 64: Flag of the Choctaw Brigade.

Another Confederate Indian flag was that of the Choctaw Brigade. Centered on the blue field of the flag was a red disk edged in white. In white silhouette on the red disk were represented traditional weapons of the Choctaw Nation—a bow, arrows, and a tomahawk.

CHAPTER 9
THE FLAG AT SEA

Navies have their own specific flags and flag terminology, and it will be helpful in understanding this chapter to be familiar with that terminology.

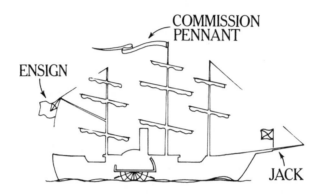

Figure 65: Illustration of a Three Masted Ship Demonstrating
Placement of the Ensign, Jack and Commission Pennant.

An ensign is the national flag as flown on a sea-going vessel. It is normally found at the stern of a ship as shown in the accompanying illustration. On special occasions a ship will be "dressed," meaning that it will be decorated with a number of national and signal flags; at such times the ensign may also be displayed at other masts. It is the custom of some nations that the ensign be of a pattern different from the national flag. A case in point is the Royal Navy of Great Britain, the ensign of which is a white flag with a red Saint George's cross and the Union flag of Britain as the canton. In America the "Stars and Stripes" evolved from the red British merchant ensign. As a result the national flag was also used as the ensign, and this practice was carried over by the Confederate States.

The other distinctively naval flags are the jack and the commission pennant. The jack is a flag, designating the nationality, which is flown from the jack staff at the bow of the ship. It is flown only on a ship of war and then only when the vessel is in port. The Royal Navy flies the canton of its white ensign as a jack, which tradition was carried over into the navies of both the United States and the Confederate States.

66

THE FLAG AT SEA

The commission pennant is flown from the main mast of a ship and designates its status as a commissioned vessel of its country's navy. This pennant may only be displayed by a ship in the national service.

The National Ensign

The ensign of the Confederate States conforms to the design of the Confederate Flag for the appropriate time period: the "Stars and Bars" from March 4, 1861 to May 1, 1863; the "Stainless Banner" from May 1, 1863 to March 4, 1865; and the last Confederate Flag after March 4, 1865.

There are no regulations extant for the ensign of 1861, and the evidence is that it conformed exactly to the national flag. Some sources have indicated that a naval ensign was used which arranged the stars in rows rather than a circle. Although a few ensigns do exist with such a star pattern, the vast majority of surviving flags have their stars in a circular arrangement.

On May 26, 1863, Secretary of the Navy Stephen R. Mallory promulgated regulations adopting a new set of naval flags to conform with the Flag Act adopted by Congress on May 1 of that year. In these regulations, Mallory modified the "Stainless Banner" for its role as a national ensign by reducing its proportional length. While the Flag Act of 1863 called for the flag's width to be half its length, the naval regulations specified a width for the ensign of two-thirds its length. A 72 inch wide ensign would have a length of 108 inches as compared to a 144 inch length for national flag of the same width.

Figure 66: Confederate States Naval Ensign
After May 26, 1863.

FLAGS OF THE CONFEDERACY

When Congress adopted the final Confederate Flag in 1865, the naval regulations should have changed to adapt to the new law, especially since the call for the change seems to have come from the navy. The new flag's overall proportions corresponded to the regulation's specifications for the ensign, and the likelihood is that the new ensign would not have varied its details from those of the national flag. No new flag regulations are know to have been adopted by the navy after the passage of the Flag Act of 1865 and, with one exception, the Confederate States Navy ceased to exist a little over two months later.

The one exception was the CSS *Shenandoah*. While Lee and Johnston were surrendering their armies, she was sinking United States ships in the North Pacific. When General Stand Watie was surrendering his Indian division on June 23, 1865, the *Shenandoah* was in the process of capturing twenty-five ships of the New Bedford whaling fleet near the Bering Strait. Only on August 2 did Captain Waddell of the *Shenandoah* receive positive information from a British ship that his government no longer existed. Determined not to surrender to the United States authorities, Waddell set course for Britain. On November 5, 1865 the *Shenandoah* arrived at the British coast where she had begun her voyage over a year before. On November 6 she sailed into Liverpool harbor, and the white ensign of the Confederate States of America was lowered for the last time.

The Confederate Jack

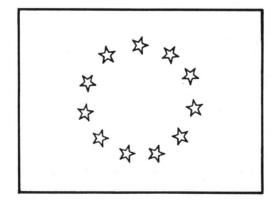

Figure 67: Confederate Navy Jack
March 4, 1861 to May 26, 1863.

THE FLAG AT SEA

As we have seen, the Confederate States followed the precedent established by Great Britain, and adopted by the United States, of using the canton of the ensign as the jack of the navy. The first Confederate jack, like the jack of the Union navy, was a blue flag on which were placed the stars corresponding with the number of States in the Confederacy.

Figure 68: Confederate Navy Jack
after May 26, 1863.

The naval flag regulations of 1863, which adopted the new national ensign, also adopted a new jack. The jack was now to be "the same as the union for the Ensign, excepting that its length shall be one and a half times its width." In design and proportions it is very similar to the battle flag issued to the Army of Tennessee in 1864. Since the Flag Act of 1865 did not change the basic design of the Confederate Flag's canton, the jack of 1863 would have remained the Confederate jack after 1865.

Commission Pennants

Naval commission pennants are designed to indicate the nationality of a ship and to indicate its commissioned status in the national service. The commission pennant of the United States Navy is blue at its head with seven white stars and has two stripes of white over red trailing out from the blue.

No published regulations exisit for the Confederate States Navy's commission pennant prior to 1863. Evidence from a surviving pennant, and from engraved plates in Admiral Raphael Semmes' book *Memoirs of Service Afloat*, however, indicates that the Confederate pennant was derived from

Figure 69: Confederate Commission Pennant,
March 4, 1861 to May 26, 1863.

that of the United States. It also had a blue head, on which was placed a star for each of the Confederate States. The stripes on this pennant were three in number and were colored red, white, and red, corresponding to the bars of the Confederate Flag.

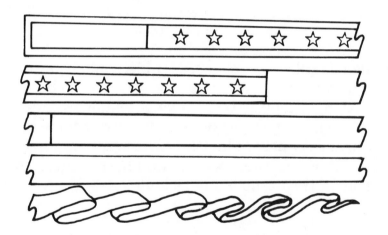

Figure 70: Confederate Commission Pennant,
After May 26, 1863.

The naval regulations of May 26, 1863 gave the Confederate States Navy a new commission pennant in keeping with the new Confederate Flag and ensign. The proportions of the pennant are dramatic with the length to be seventy-two times the width at the head and tapering to a point. The first portion of the pennant is red, edged in white on the outer edges, with a length three times the width at the head. It is followed by a white edged, blue section twelve times longer than the width of the pennant, and decorated with stars equal in number to the States in the Confederacy. This is followed by an unbordered red section, the same length as the first red section, and the remaining three-fourths of the pennant is white.

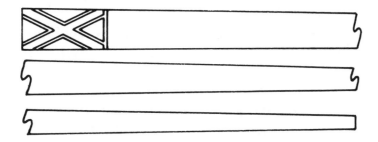

Figure 71: Variant Confederate Commission Pennant Used
After May 1, 1863.

Other commission pennants of a non-regulation character were used from time to time during the course of the War. One such example is also influenced by the Confederate Flag of 1863, but is not much influenced by the official navy regulations. Rather than having the red-blue-red sections of the official pennant, the head of this variant is in the form of the "Southern Cross" union of the ensign with the stars omitted.

The Revenue Service

The United States Revenue Service was created in the early years of the Union to collect import duties and to protect the coasts against smugglers trying to evade duties and taxes. The United States Navy was unable to

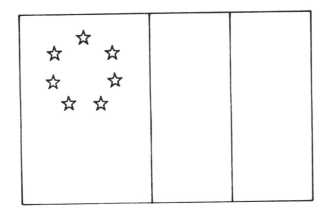

Figure 72: Confederate States Revenue Service Ensign.

provide this service while off fighting quasi-wars in European waters or pirates on the Barbary Coast. Congress, therefore, created the Revenue Service as a branch of the Treasury Department and authorized its use of ships to serve as revenue cutters.

When the Confederate States government was established, all laws of the United States which were not inconsistent with the Confederate Constitution were made laws of the Confederacy. These included the law establishing the Revenue Service, and the Confederate States Treasury Department's Revenue Service functioned in much the same way as did that of the United States. Among the privileges of the Revenue Service was that of lying its own distinctive ensign from its vessels. The ensign of the U.S. Revenue Service altered the U.S. ensign by displaying vertical stripes. Its canton was white with blue stars and the arms of the United States.

The Confederate States Revenue Service did not copy the white canton of its predecessor's ensign, but it did follow the scheme of vertical stripes and applied it to the "Stars and Bars" flag of the Confederacy. The canton was extended the entire width of the ensign, and one of its red bars was pivoted to a vertical position; the other red bar was eliminated. The resulting ensign looked very much like a French flag with a circle of stars in the upper part of the blue bar. As a rule, the blue bar was wider than the white or red bars by about one and a half times.

EPILOGUE

THE CONFEDERATE STATES OF AMERICA died a violent death at the hands of invading armies in 1865, and thus it was "proven" that secession was wrong . . . that no portion of the American people could elect a path of political self-determination so long as a more powerful section opposed them. The flags which represented the national aspirations of the Southern people were buried in the archives of the conquerors, until President Theodore Roosevelt had them returned to the people whose hopes had once been swaddled in their folds. During the time of obscurity the memory of them dimmed, and many errors have persisted about their design and usage. Over one hundred twenty-five years later, revisionists attempt to distort their meaning and place in history.

The flags of the Confederacy represented the aspirations of a brave and resourceful people who determined to strike out on their own and carve their place among the nations of the earth. Their desire to live under a government based upon "the consent of the governed" should be respected; and their tenacity in attempting to preserve their chosen government, though in vain, must be admired. The people of the Confederate States of America earned for their flags an honored place among the sacred relics of human endeavor.

FURTHER READING

Other books are available for further study of Confederate flags and of flags in general. A very detailed study of a large number of individual Confederate flags has been carried out by Howard Michael Madaus of the Milwaukee Public Museum. The results of his research has been published in the following works:

Madaus, Howard Michael. *The Battle Flags of the Confederate Army of Tennessee.* Milwaukee Wisc.: Milwaukee Public Museum, 1976.

_____. "Rebel Flags Afloat." *The Flag Bulletin,* Vol. XXV, No. 1. Winchester, Mass.: The Flag Research Center, 1986.

_____. *The Southern Cross.* [an unpublished manuscript scheduled for publication in late 1988].

For general works on flags the reader may refer to any number of references. Two of these have been written by the director of the Flag Research Center

Smith, Whitney. *The Flag Book of the United States.* New York: William Morrow & Company, Inc., 1970.

_____. *Flags Through the Ages and Across the World.* New York: McGraw-Hill, 1975.

The Flag Research Center publishes a bi-monthly journal called *The Flag Bulletin,* which is available from the Flag Research Center, 3 Edgehill Road, Winchester, Mass. 01890.

Further reading and research into the actions of the Confederate States Congress on flag and other matters may be had in a number of works. Those which would qualify as primary source materials are:

Matthews, James A., ed. *Statutes at Large of the Provisional Government of the Confederate States of America.* Richmond, Va.: R.M. Smith, 1864.

_____. *Statutes at Large of the Confederate States of America Passed at the First Session of the First Congress.* Richmond, Va.: R.M. Smith, 1862.

_____. *Statutes at Large of the Confederate States of America Passed at the Second Session of the First Congress.* Richmond, Va.: R.M. Smith, 1862.

_____. *Statutes at Large of the Confederate States of America Passed at the Third Session of the First Congress.* Richmond, Va.: R.M. Smith, 1863.

_____. *Statutes at Large of the Confederate States of America Passed at the Fourth Session of the First Congress.* Richmond Va.: R.M. Smith, 1864.

_____. *Statutes at Large of the Confederate States of America Passed at the First Session of the Second Congress.* Richmond Va.: R.M. Smith, 1864.

Journal of the Congress of the Confederate States of America, 1861-1865, Washington, D.C.: Government Printing Office, 1904.

Freeman, Douglas Southall, ed. "Proceeding of the Confederate Congress." *The Southern Historical Society Papers.* Vols. 44-52. Richmond, Va.: Southern Historical Society, 1923-1959.

APPENDIX A - CHRONOLOGY

1860

November 6: Presidential election results in Republican electors gaining a majority in the Electoral College.

November 13: South Carolina legislature passes an act calling for the assembly of a convention to consider secession.

December 6: The Electoral College elects Abraham Lincoln President of the United States of America.

December 17: South Carolina Convention assembles in Columbia.

December 18: Outbreak of smallpox causes the Convention to adjourn to Charleston.

December 20: South Carolina Convention adopts the Ordinance of Secession.

1861

January 9: Mississippi Secession Convention adopts an Ordinance of Secession.

January 10: Florida Secession Convention adopts an Ordinance of Secession.

January 11: Alabama Secession Convention adopts an Ordinance of Secession; Alabama State flag is raised at capitol in Montgomery.

January 13: Commanding general of the Florida military adopts a provisional flag for Florida.

January 19: Georgia Secession Convention adopts an Ordinance of Secession; Georgia flag is raised over capitol at Milledgeville.

APPENDIX A - CHRONOLOGY

January 26: Louisiana Secession Convention adopts an Ordinance of Secession; Pelican flag is raised at the Louisiana Secession Hall; Mississippi adopts an official State flag.

February 4: Texas Secession Convention adopts an Ordinance of Secession and submits it to a vote of the people.

February 4: Delegates of six seceded States assemble in Convention in Montgomery, Alabama.

February 8: The Montgomery Convention adopts a Constitution forming the Provisional Government of the Confederate States of America.

February 11: Louisiana adopts an official State flag.

February 18: Jefferson Davis is inaugurated President of the Provisional Government of the Confederate States.

February 23: The people of Texas ratify the Ordinance of Secession.

March 2: Texas secession becomes official. The Confederate Congress passes "An Act to admit Texas as a Member of the Confederate States of America."

March 4: The first Confederate Flag adopted and raised over the Alabama capitol.

March 11: The Confederate Convention adopts the Constitution of the Confederate States of America.

March 12: Alabama ratifies the C.S. Constitution.

March 16: Georgia ratifies the C.S. Constitution. March 21: Louisiana ratifies the C.S. Constitution.

March 23: Texas ratifies the C.S. Constitution.

March 26: Mississippi ratifies the C.S. Constitution

April 3: South Carolina ratifies the C.S. Constitution.

APPENDIX A - CHRONOLOGY

April 12: The bombardment of Fort Sumter.

April 15: Lincoln issues call for 75,000 troops to serve three months.

April 17: Virginia Secession Convention adopts an Ordinance of Secession.

April 19: Lincoln announces the blockade of Southern ports.

April 22: Florida ratifies the C.S. Constitution.

April 25: A resolution introduced in Tennessee Senate proposing a State flag.

April 30: Virginia adopts an official State flag.

May 6: Arkansas Secession Convention adopts an Ordinance of Secession; Confederate Congress passes "An act recognizing the existence of war between the United States and the Confederate States;" Tennessee legislature adopts a Declaration of Independence to be submitted to a popular vote.

May 7: Tennessee legislature ratifies a military league with the Confederate States; Virginia admitted to the Confederacy.

May 20: North Carolina Convention adopts an Ordinance of Secession.

May 21: Arkansas admitted to the Confederacy.

May 24: Resolution of neutrality adopted by Kentucky; United States troops invade Virginia.

June 1: Arkansas ratifies the C.S. Constitution.

June 6: North Carolina ratifies the C.S. Constitution.

June 8: Tennessee voters ratify the Declaration of Independence.

June 19: Virginia ratifies the C.S. Constitution.

June 22: North Carolina adopts official State flag.

APPENDIX A - CHRONOLOGY

June 24: Governor Isham G. Harris proclaims Tennessee officially out of the Union.

July 2: North Carolina and Tennessee admitted to the Confederacy.

July 10: Confederate States sign treaty with the Creek Nation.

July 12: Confederate States sign treaty with the Choctaw and Chickasaw Nations.

July 21: Battle of Manassas in Virginia.

August 1: Tennessee voters ratify the C.S. Constitution; Confederate States sign a treaty with the Seminole Nation.

August 5: Governor Claiborne F. Jackson declares the independence of Missouri.

August 12: Confederate States sign a treaty with the Pen-e-tegh-ca Band of the Commanches, and the tribes and bands of the Wichitas, A-na-dagh-cos, Ton-ca-wes, Ai-o-nais, Ki-Chais, Shawnees and Delawares; Confederate States sign a treaty with the Commanches of the Prairies and Staked Plains.

September: The "Southern Cross" battle flag is adopted for use by the Confederate Army of the Potomac in Virginia.

September 13: Florida adopts an official State flag.

October 2: Confederate States sign a treaty with the Great Osage Tribe.

October 4: Confederate States sign a treaty with the Seneca and Shawnee Tribes; Confederate States sign a treaty with the Quapaw Tribe.

October 7: Confederate States sign a treaty with the Cherokee Nation.

October 31: Missouri legislature adopts an Act of Secession.

November: First "Southern Cross" battle flags issued to the Confederate army in Virginia.

APPENDIX A - CHRONOLOGY

November 6: First general elections for members of the Confederate Presidential Electoral College and C.S. House of Representatives.

November 20: Kentucky Secession Convention adopts an Ordinance of Secession.

November 28: Missouri admitted to the Confederacy.

December 6: Confederate Electoral College elects Jefferson Davis President of the Confederate States of America.

December 10: Kentucky admitted to the Confederacy.

1862

January 19-20: Battle of Mill Springs, Kentucky.

February 6: Fort Henry in Tennessee falls to Union forces.

February 16: Fort Donelson in Tennessee is surrendered.

February 18: First Congress of the Confederate States convenes.

February 22: Jefferson Davis inaugurated President of the Confederate States.

February 23: Nashville, Tennessee is evacuated.

March 6-8: Battle of Pea Ridge, Arkansas.

March 9: Battle of Hampton Roads, Virginia between CSS *Virginia* (formerly *Merrimac)* and USS *Monitor.*

April 6-7: Battle of Shiloh, Tennessee.

April 19: Joint Committee on Flag and Seal proposes a new Confederate flag.

APPENDIX A - CHRONOLOGY

April 24: New Orleans is captured.

May 31: Battle of Seven Pines in Virginia.

June 6: Memphis, Tennessee is captured.

June 26: The Seven Days Battle begins in Virginia.

July 1: Battle of Malvern Hill in Virginia.

July 13: Forrest captures Union garrison at Murfreesboro, Tennessee.

August 9: Battle of Cedar Mountain, Virginia.

August 30: Second Battle of Manassas in Virginia.

September 16-17: Battle of Sharpsburg, Maryland.

October 3-4: Battle of Corinth, Mississippi.

October 8: Battle of Perryville, Kentucky.

November: 20 The Army of the Mississippi is re-named The Army of Tennessee.

December 31: The Battle of Murfreesboro (Stones River) in Tennessee begins.

1863

January 1: Union forces driven from Galveston, Texas.

April 22: C.S. Senate passes Senate Bill No. 132 to propose a new Confederate Flag.

May 1: The Flag Act of 1863 establishes the "Stainless Banner" as the Confederate Flag.

APPENDIX A - CHRONOLOGY

May 1-4: Battle of Chancellorsville, Virginia.

May 10: Stonewall Jackson dies.

May 14: Union forces capture Jackson, Mississippi.

May 26: Secretary of Navy Mallory issues regulations adopting a new ensign, jack and commission pennant for the Confederate States Navy.

July 1-3: Battle of Gettysburg, Pennsylvania.

July 4: Fall of Vicksburg, Mississippi.

September 19-20: Battle of Chickamauga, Georgia.

October 25: Battle of Pine Bluff, Arkansas.

November 23-25: Battles of Chattanooga, Lookout Mountain and Missionary Ridge, Tennessee.

December 18: General Joseph E. Johnston takes command of the Army of Tennessee.

1864

February 20: Battle of Olustee, Florida.

March & April: New "Southern Cross" battle flags issued to the Army of Tennessee.

March 8-9: Union Red River expedition in Louisiana defeated.

March 12: Battle of Fort Pillow, Tennessee.

May 5-7: Battle of the Wilderness in Virginia.

May 13-16: Battle of Resaca, Georgia.

May 15: Battle of New Market, Virginia.

APPENDIX A - CHRONOLOGY

June 1-3: Battle of Cold Harbor, Virginia.

June 10: Battle of Brice's Crossroads, Mississippi.

June 27: Battle of Kennesaw Mountain, Georgia.

July 22: Battle of Atlanta, Georgia.

August 5: Battle of Jonesboro, Georgia.

September 2: Sherman takes Atlanta.

October 8: CSS *Shenandoah* commissioned.

November 30: Battle of Franklin, Tennessee.

December 15-16: Battle of Nashville, Tennessee.

December 22: Savannah, Georgia evacuated.

1865

January 15: Fort Fisher, North Carolina falls.

February 17: Sherman captures and burns Columbia, South Carolina.

March 4: Flag Act of 1865 establishes the last Confederate Flag.

March 19-20: Battle of Bentonville, North Carolina.

April 1: Battle of Five Forks in Virginia.

April 2: Richmond and Petersburg evacuated.

April 9: Lee surrenders the Army of Northern Virginia.

April 12: Mobile, Alabama is captured.

APPENDIX A - CHRONOLOGY

April 13: Montgomery, Alabama is captured.

April 26: Johnston surrenders the Army of Tennessee.

May 4: The Department of Alabama Mississippi and East Louisiana is surrendered.

May 13: The last battle is fought at Palmetto Ranch near Brownsville, Texas.

May 23: The Army of the Trans-Mississippi Department is surrendered.

June 2: Galveston, Texas surrenders.

June 23: General Stand Watie surrenders his Indian Division.

June 28: CSS *Shenandoah* fires the last shots of the War.

July 4: General Jo Shelby crosses into Mexico.

July 14: Governor of the Chickasaw Nation ends resistance to the United States.

November 6: CSS *Shenandoah* lowers the last Confederate Flag at Liverpool, England.

APPENDIX B
CONFEDERATE FLAG LAWS

1861

STARS AND BARS

Mr. Miles, from the Committee on the Flag and Seal of the Confederacy, made the following report:

The committee appointed to select a proper flag for the Confederate States of America, beg leave to report:

That they have given this subject due consideration, and carefully inspected all the designs and models submitted to them. The number of these has been immense, but they all may be divided into two great classes.

First. Those which copy and preserve the principal features of the United States flag, with slight and unimportant modifications.

Secondly. Those which are very elaborate, complicated, or fantastical. The objection to the first class is, that none of them at any considerable distance could readily be distinguished from the one which they imitate. Whatever attachment may be felt, from association, for the "Stars and Stripes" (an attachment which your committee may be permitted to say they do not all share), it is manifest that in inaugurating a new government we can not with any propriety, or without encountering very obvious practical difficulties, retain the flag of the Government from which we have withdrawn. There is no propriety in retaining the ensign of a government which, in the opinion of the States composing this Confederacy, had become so oppressive and injurious to their interests as to require their separation from it. It is idle to talk of "keeping" the flag of the United States when we have voluntarily seceded from them. It is superfluous to dwell upon the practical difficulties which would flow from the fact of two distinct and probably hostile governments, both employing the same or very similar flags. It would be a political and military solecism. It would lead to perpetual disputes. As to "the glories of the old flag," we must bear in mind that the battles of the Revolution, about which our fondest and proudest memories cluster, were not fought beneath its folds. And although in more recent times — in the war of 1812 and in the war with Mexico — the South did win her fair share of glory, and shed her full measure of blood under its guidance and in its defense, we think the impartial page of history will preserve and commemorate the fact more imperishably than a mere piece of striped bunting. When the colonies achieved their independence of the "mother country" (which up to the last they fondly called her) they did not desire to retain the British flag or anything at all similar to it. Yet, under that flag they had been planted, and nurtured, and fostered. Under that flag they had fought in their infancy for their very existence against more than one determined foe; under it they had repelled and driven back the relentless savage, and carried it farther and farther into the decreasing wilderness as the standard of civilization and religion; under it the youthful Washington won his spurs in the memorable and unfortunate expedition of Braddock, and Americans helped to plant it on the heights of Abraham, where the immortal Wolfe fell, covered with glory, in the arms of victory. But our forefathers, when they separated themselves from Great Britain — a separation not on account of their hatred of the English constitution or of English institutions, but in consequence of the tyrannical and unconstitutional rule of Lord North's administration, and because their destiny beckoned them on to independent expansion and achievement — cast no lingering, regretful looks behind. They were proud of their race and lineage, proud of their heritage in the glories and genius and language of old England, but they were influenced by the spirit and the motto of the great Hampden, *"vestigia nulla retrorsum,"* They were determined to build up a new power among the nations of the world. They therefore did not attempt "to keep the old flag." We think it is good to imitate them in this comparatively lively little matter as well as to emulate them in greater and more important ones.

The committee, in examining the representations of the flags of all countries, found that Liberia and the Sandwich Islands had flags so similar to that of the United States that it seemed to them an additional, if not itself a conclusive, reason why we should not "keep," copy, or imitate it. They felt no inclination to borrow, at second hand, what had been pilfered and appropriated by a free negro community and a race of savages. It must be admitted, however, that something was conceded by the committee to what seemed so strong and earnest a desire to retain at least a suggestion of the old "Stars and Stripes." So much for the mass of models and designs more or less copied from, or assimilated to, the United States flag.

With reference to the second class of designs - those of an elaborate and complicated character (but many of them showing considerable artistic skill and taste) — the committee will merely remark, that however pretty they may be, when made up by the cunning skill of a fair lady's fingers in silk, satin, and embroidery, they are not appropriate as flags. A flag should be simple, readily made, and, above all, capable of being made up in bunting. It should be different from the flag of any other country, place, or people. It should be readily distinguishable at a distance. The colors should be well contrasted and durable, and, lastly, and not the least important point, it should be effective and handsome.

The committee humbly think that the flag which they submit combines these requisites It is very easy to make. It is entirely different from any national flag. The three colors of which it is composed — red, white, and blue — are the true republican colors. In heraldry they are emblematic of the three great virtues — of valor, purity, and truth. Naval men assure us that it can be recognized and distinguished at a great distance. The colors contrast admirably and are lasting. In effect and appearance it must speak for itself.

Your committee, therefore, recommend that the flag of the Confederate States of America shall consist of a red field with a white space extending horizontally through the center, and equal in width to one-third the width of the flag. The red spaces above and below to be the same width as the white. The union blue extending down through the white space and stopping at the lower red space. In the center of the union a circle of white stars corresponding in number with the States of the Confederacy. If adopted, long may it wave over a brave, a free, and a virtuous people. May the career of the Confederacy, whose duty it will then be to support and defend it, be such as to endear it to our children's children, as the flag of a loved, because just and benign, government, and the cherished symbol of its valor, purity, and truth.

Respectfully submitted.
Wm. Porcher Miles,
Chairman

1863
FLAG ACT OF 1863

ACT to establish the flag of the
Confederate States

The Congress of the Confederate States of America do enact, That the flag of the Confederate States shall be as follows: The field to be white, the length double the width of the flag, with the union (now used as the battle flag) to be a square of two-thirds the width of the flag, having the ground red, thereupon a broad saltier of blue, bordered with white and emblazoned with mullets or five-pointed stars, corresponding in number to that of the Confederate States.

Approved May 1, 1863

NAVY REGULATIONS OF 1863

The new Ensign, Pennant, and Jack, by order of the Secretary of the Navy, May 26, 1863, as follows:

THE NEW ENSIGN.

The new Ensign will be made according to the following directions,

The field to be white, the length one and a half times the width of the flag, with the union (now used as the Battle Flag) to be square, of two-thirds of the width of the flag, having the ground red, thereon a broad saltier of blue, to the union as 1 : 4 4/5, bordered with white, to the union as 1 : 22, and emblazoned with white mullets, or five-pointed stars, diameter of stars to the union as 1 : 6 2/5 corresponding in number to that of the Confederate States.

THE PENNANT.

A white ground, its size to be as 1 : 72, or its length seventy-two times its width at the head, and tapering to a point.

The union of the Pennant to be as follows: All red from the head for three times its width, with a white border equal to half its width, then all blue in length equal to twelve times its width, to be emblazoned with stars, in number equal to those in the Ensign, with a white border equal to half the width, and then red three times the width, with the fly all white.

THE JACK.

To be the same as the union for the Ensign, except that its length shall be one and a half times its width.

1865
FLAG ACT OF 1865

AN ACT to establish the flag of the
Confederate States.

The Congress of the Confederate States of America do enact, That the flag of the Confederate States of America shall be as follows: The width two-thirds of its length, with the union (now used as the battle flag) to be in width three-fifths of the width of the flag, and so proportioned as to leave the length of the field on the side of the union twice the width of the field below it; to have the ground red and a broad saltier thereon, bordered with white and emblazoned with mullets or five-pointed stars, corresponding in number to that of the Confederate States; the field to be white, except the outer half from the union to be a red bar extending the width of the flag.

Approved March 4, 1865

APPENDIX C

CONFEDERATE FLAG DAY
AND
THE SALUTE TO THE CONFEDERATE FLAG.

CONFEDERATE FLAG DAY

In recent years efforts have been undertaken by various Confederate hereditary and patriotic organizations to promote a greater knowledge of and respect for the flags of the Confederate States. This activity has increased since the 125th anniversary of the adoption of the first Confederate Flag occurred on March 4, 1986. One form which this effort has taken is the recognition of Confederate Flag Day.

The first formal acknowledgment of Confederate Flag Day was a resolution adopted by the Tennessee Division of the Sons of Confederate Veterans. At their 1987 State Convention a motion was passed to declare the fourth day of March in each year as Confederate Flag Day in the State of Tennessee. March 4 was chosen because it marked the common date of the adoption of the first Confederate Flag in 1861 and of the last Confederate Flag in 1865.

SALUTE TO THE CONFEDERATE FLAG.

In the early days of the Confederate veterans' and descendants' organizations, a salute to the flag of the Confederate States was adopted. This is not a pledge of allegiance, but rather, an affectionate greeting to the emblem of a Cause fondly remembered.

> I salute the Confederate Flag
> with affection, reverence, and
> undying devotion to the Cause
> for which it stands.

To
Albert G. Pike, Esq.,
The Poet Lawyer of Arkansas

THE

BONNIE BLUE FLAG

COMPOSED, ARRANGED,
And Sung
AT HIS

PERSONATION ... CONCERTS
BY

HARRY MACARTHY.
THE ARKANSAS COMEDIAN.

NEW ORLEANS
Published by A.E. BLACKMAR & BRO. 74. Camp St.

THE BONNIE BLUE FLAG.

Words by
HARRY MACARTHY

Music by
VALENTINE VOUSDEN

THE BONNIE BLUE FLAG.

trea - sure, blood and toil; And when our rights were threaten'd, The cry rose near and

far,......... Hur-rah for the Bonnie Blue Flag, that bears a Sin - gle Star!

CHORUS.

Hur - rah !........ Hur - rah !........ for South- ern Rights hur - rah !........ Hur- rah ! for the

Bonnie Blue Flag that bears a Sin-gle Star..........

THE BONNIE BLUE FLAG.

SECOND VERSE.

As long as the Un-ion was faithful to her trust, Like friends and like breth-er-en, kind were we and just; But now when Northern treach-er-y at-tempts our rights to mar, We hoist on high the Bonnie Blue Flag that bears a Sin-gle Star.

3 First, gallant South Carolina nobly made the stand;
Then came Alabama, who took her by the hand;
Next, quickly Mississippi, Georgia and Florida,
All rais'd on high the Bonnie Blue Flag that bears a Single Star.

4 Ye men of valor, gather round the Banner of the Right,
Texas and fair Louisiana, join us in the fight;
Davis, our loved President, and Stephens, Stateman rare,
Now rally round the Bonnie Blue Flag that bears a Single Star.

5 And here's to brave Virginia! the Old Dominion State
With the young Confederacy at length has linked her fate;
Impell'd by her example, now other State prepare
To hoist on high the Bonnie Blue Flag that bears a Single Star.

6 Then cheer, boys, raise the joyous shout,
For Arkansas and North Carolina now have both gone out;
And let another rousing cheer for Tennessee be given,
The Single Star of the Bonnie Blue Flag has grown to be Eleven.

7 Then here's to our Confederacy, strong we are and brave,
Like patriots of old, we'll fight our heritage to save;
And rather than submit to shame, to die we would prefer,
So cheer for the Bonnie Blue Flag that bears a Single Star.

CHORUS.—Hurrah! Hurrah! for Southern Rights, hurrah!
Hurrah! for the Bonnie Blue Flag has gain'd th' Eleventh Star!

INDEX

-A-

Alabama, 31, 37-38, 46, 60
Alabama Department of Archives and History, 11
Alabama legislature, 11-12
Alabama Secession Convention, 37
Alabama State flag, 7, 37-38
Appomatox Court House, 54
Arizona, 61
Arkansas, 10, 48, 61
Army of Kentucky, 59
Army of Northern Virginia, 16, 18, 51-54, 62
Army of Tennessee, 57-58, 60, 62, 69
Army of the Mississippi, 56-57
Army of the Potomac, 51
Army of the West, 63

-B-

Barksdale, Ethelbert, 17
Beauregard, P. G. T, 7, 8, 51-52, 54-56, 59, 63
Bonnie Blue flag, 31-33, 35, 37, 42, 43-44, 45
Bragg, Braxton, 56, 57, 59
Breckinridge, John C., 56
British America, 25
British red ensign, 25-26, 28, 66
British Union flag, 25, 28
British white ensign, 66
Brown, Albert, 22

-C-

Cedar Mountain, 54
Chancellorsville, 19, 54
Charleston, 10, 35
Chattanooga, 57
Cherokee Nation, 61-62, 64
Chickasaw Nation, 61-62
Choctaw Brigade, 65
Choctaw Nation, 61-65
Cleburne, Patrick R., 57
Coahuila, 62
Colbert, Winchester, 62
Cold Harbor, 54
Commission pennant, 67, 69-71

Committee on Flag and Seal, C.S. House of Representatives, 23
Committee on Flag and Seal, C.S. Senate, 6
Committee on Flag and Seal, Provisional Congress, 7, 9, 12
Conrad, Charles M., 15
Constitution, Confederate States, 2
Constitution, United States, 1, 2
Continental Congress, 26, 27
Creek Nation, 61

-D-

Davis, Jefferson, 2, 7, 19, 23, 39
Declaration of Independence, Texas, 41
Declaration of Independence, United States, 26
de Lassus, Governor of West Florida, 31-32
Department of Alabama, Mississippi and East Louisiana, 60-61
Department of South Carolina, Georgia and Florida, 58-59

-E-

East Florida, 31
East Tennessee, Department of, 59-60
Episcopal Church, 56

-F-

Federal Republic of America, 2
First Arkansas Cavalry, 63
First Cherokee Mounted Rifles, 64
First Congress, 2, 14, 18
Flag Act of 1863, 20, 22, 67
Flag Act of 1865, 23, 68, 69
Florida, 36-37, 46, 59
Florida, Military Department, 37
Florida, provisional flag, 36-37
Florida, State flag, 36-37
Forrest, Nathan Bedford, 61
Fort Moultrie, 34
Fort Sumter, 10
France, 31, 41
French Bourbon flag, 18, 22

-G-

Georgia, 39, 59
Georgia State flag, 7, 39
Gettysburg, 54
Gray, Peter W., 19
Grand Union flag, 26, 28
Great Britain, 25, 46, 69

-H-

Hardee, William J., 55, 58
House of Representatives, C.S., 14, 19, 23
Houston, 19

-J-

Jackson flag, 20
Jackson, Thomas J. "Stonewall", 19-20
James I of England, 25
James VI of Scotland, 25
Johnson, Issac, 31
Johnson, Mellisa, 32
Johnston, Albert Sidney, 54-55
Johnston, Joseph E., 51-52, 57, 68
Joint Committee on Flag and Seal, 14
Jones, John Paul, 26

-K-

Kemper, Nathan, 31
Kemper Rebellion, 31
Kemper, Reuben, 31
Kemper, Sam, 31
Kentucky, 10, 13, 47-48
Kentucky legislature, 47
Kentucky, provisional government, 47-48
Kentucky Secession Convention, 47
Kentucky State seal, 47-48
King's Colors, 51

-L-

Lee, Robert E., 22, 51, 54, 68
Lincoln, Abraham, 7
Liverpool, 68
Louisiana, 31, 40-41, 46, 60, 61, 62

Louisiana Secession Convention, 40
Louisiana State flag, 40-41

-M-

Macarthy, Harry, 31, 32
Madaus, Howard Michael, 12
Madison, James, 32
Magnolia flag, 36
Mallory, Stephen R., 67
Manassas, 51
Marschall, Nicola, 10-11
Mecklenburg Resolves, 45
Mexican Constitution of 1824, 41
Mexico, 41, 62
Miles, William Porcher, 7, 8, 9, 14-15, 18,
    22, 51-52
Military Committee, C.S. Senate, 23
Milwaukee Public Museum, 12
Mississippi, 31-32, 35-36, 46, 60
Mississippi River, 31, 60, 61
Mississippi Secession Convention, 31
Mississippi State flag, 35, 36
Missouri, 10, 13, 48, 52, 61, 62, 64
Missouri battle flag, 64
Missouri State flag, 48
Mobile, 60
Montgomery, 2, 7, 9, 10
Museum of the Confederacy, 20, 39

-N-

Naval Committee, C.S. Senate, 22
Naval ensign, 20, 67-68
Naval jack, 66, 68-69
Newman, Tazewell W., 46-47
North Carolina, 10, 45-46
North Carolina Secession Convention, 45
North Carolina State flag, 45-46

-O-

Oklahoma, 61

-P-

Palmetto flag, 35
Parson's Texas Cavalry Brigade, 62

Pelican flag, 40
Petersburg, 54
Pike, Albert, 64
Polk, Leonidas, 55-56, 63
Price, Sterling, 48
Provisional Congress, 2, 7-11

-R-

Revenue Service, C.S., 72
Revenue Service, U.S., 71-72
Revolutionary War, 34-35
Rhea, John, 32
Richmond, 11, 14, 61
Rio Grande, 62
Roosevelt, Theodore, 73
Ross, John, 64
Royal Navy, 66

-S-

Saint Andrew's cross, 18, 60
Saint Andrew's flag, 25
Saint George's cross, 8, 56, 63, 66
Saint George's flag, 25
Scotland, 25, 60
Second Congress, 2, 22-23
Secretary of War, U.S., 44
Seminole Nation, 61
Semmes, Raphael, 69
Semmes, Thomas J., 22
Senate Bill No. 132, 16-19
Senate Bill No. 137, 22-23
Senate, C.S., 14-17, 19, 22-23
Senate Resolution No. 2, 46
Senate Resolution No. 11, 15
Sharpsburg, 54
Shelby, Jo, 61-62
Shenandoah, C.S.S., 8, 68
Shiloh, 57
Smith, Orren Randolph, 10-11
Sons of Confederate Veterans, 47
South Carolina, 34-35, 59
South Carolina Secession Convention, 8
South Carolina State flag, 34-35
South Carolina State seal, 35
Southern Cross, 52, 54, 55, 57-58, 59, 60,
    62, 71

Spain, 31-32, 41
Sparrow, Edward, 22
Stainless Banner, 14-21, 28, 67
Stars and Bars, 7-13, 14, 16, 20, 23, 27, 28,
    47, 51, 57, 67, 72
Stars and Stripes, 14, 16, 26, 28, 51, 66
Swan, William G., 17-18

-T-

Taylor, Richard, 62
Tennessee, 10, 13, 46-47
Tennessee General Assembly, 46-47
Tennessee State flag, 46
Tennessee State seal, 46-47
Texas, 31, 34, 41-44, 46, 62
Texas civil ensign, 44
Texas national flag, 31, 41-42
Texas naval ensign, 43
Texas State flag, 42-43
Thomas, Philemon, 32
Trans-Mississippi Department, 61-65
Trippe, Robert P., 18
Tyler, John, 9
Tyler, Letitia Christian, 9

-U-

Union flag , 25, 28, 66
United Confederate Veterans, 11-12
United Kingdom, 25

-V-

Van Dorn, Earl, 52, 63
Virginia, 10, 15, 34, 44-45
Virginia State flag, 44-45
Virginia State seal, 44-45

-W-

Waddell, James I., 68
Washington, George, 26
Washington, Republic of, 2
Watie, Stand, 62, 68
West Florida, 31-32, 42